THE SUM OF US

HEATHER McGHEE

THE SUM OF US

HOW RACISM HURTS EVERYONE

ADAPTED FOR YOUNG READERS

DELACORTE PRESS

The Sum of Us is a work of nonfiction. Some names and identifying details have been changed.

Text copyright © 2023 by Heather McGhee

All rights reserved. Published in the United States by Delacorte Press, an imprint of Random House Children's Books, a division of Penguin Random House LLC, New York.

This work is based on *The Sum of Us: What Racism Costs Everyone and How We Can Prosper Together*, copyright © 2021 by Heather McGhee. Published in hardcover in the United States by One World, an imprint of Random House, a division of Penguin Random House LLC, in 2021.

Delacorte Press is a registered trademark and the colophon is a trademark of Penguin Random House LLC.

Visit us on the Web! rhcbooks.com

Educators and librarians, for a variety of teaching tools, visit us at RHTeachersLibrarians.com

Library of Congress Control Number: 2022948140
ISBN 978-0-593-56262-8 (trade) — ISBN 978-0-593-56263-5 (lib. bdg.) — ISBN 978-0-593-56264-2 (ebook)

The text of this book is set in 12-point Adobe Caslon Pro.
Interior design by Cathy Bobak
Cover art by David McConochie

Printed in the United States of America
10 9 8 7 6 5 4 3
First Edition

FOR MY MOTHER

CONTENTS

INTRODUCTION

"Why can't we have nice things?"

Have you ever asked this question? By "nice things," I don't mean hovercraft or laundry that does itself. I mean the more basic aspects of a high-functioning society, like a great public school in every neighborhood, debt-free college education, affordable health care, jobs that keep people above poverty. The "we" who can't seem to have nice things is Americans, all Americans. This includes the white Americans who are the largest group of the uninsured and the impoverished. Americans of color are disproportionately impoverished and uninsured as well. "We" is all of us who have watched generations of American leadership struggle to solve big problems and reliably improve the quality of life for most people. We know what we need—why can't we have it?

"Why can't we have nice things?" was a question that struck me pretty early on in life—growing up in an era of rising inequality, seeing the wealthy neighborhoods boom while the schools and parks where most of us lived fell apart. I went on to a career in public policy advocacy, using statistical research, congressional testimony, legislative drafting, and talking to the media to advocate, basically, for more nice things for more people. I felt like I was fighting the good fight in a country where one percent of the population owned more wealth than the entire middle class while half of adult workers were paid too little to meet their basic needs for things like housing and food. But we weren't making progress fast enough, and so I decided to hit the road to find out what was holding us back.

What I found is that there are hidden costs of racism to all of us. I traveled to Mississippi and sat with factory workers trying to unite a multiracial workforce to bargain collectively for better pay and benefits. I talked to white homeowners who had lost everything in a financial crisis sparked by predatory mortgages that banks first created to strip wealth from black and brown families. I heard from white parents and students who feared that segregated white schools would render them ill-equipped for a diverse world. To understand when the majority of white Americans had turned against government solutions, I traveled to one of the many towns that had drained its public swimming pool rather than integrate it.

I didn't set out to write a book about history, but my journey revealed that a people who have been robbed of their history can be manipulated by the same forces generation after generation. Did you know that in a recent survey, less than ten percent of high school seniors could accurately say that slavery was the primary cause of the Civil War? I met a white suburban mother named Rachel who told me about her "outrage" that even though she'd been educated in Oklahoma public schools her whole life, she had only recently learned about the 1921 Tulsa Race Massacre. She recalled seeing a black Tulsa neighborhood as a child and having no answer for why it seemed so poor. In the absence of history, negative stereotypes filled the void. "What if people had been taught about why black communities were so marginalized?" she asked, her anger audible. "A chance to fully understand something was taken away from me because I didn't learn about this moment. There was this flourishing black community and we were never aware of it, because that history was robbed from me." Learning about racist episodes in history isn't racist; it's essential to erasing racism from our future.

To this day, a self-interested elite is trying to rob us of our shared history, hoping to keep people who have a lot in common from rising up together. But not everyone is buying it. Everywhere I went, I found that the people who had linked arms with others across racial lines had found the key to unlocking what I began to call a "Solidarity Dividend," from higher wages to cleaner air, made possible through multiracial collective action.

Nothing about our situation is inevitable, but you can't solve a problem with the same consciousness that created it. The outdated belief that some groups of people are better than others distorts our politics, drains our economy, and erodes everything Americans have in common, from our schools to our air to our infrastructure. Join me on a journey to understand how this idea came to be so powerful and how a new generation of cross-racial movements are working to end it, once and for all.

CHAPTER 1

AN OLD STORY: THE ZERO-SUM HIERARCHY

WHEN I WAS GROWING UP, MY FAMILY AND MY NEIGHBORS were always hustling. My mother had the fluctuating income of a person with an entrepreneur's mind and a social worker's heart. My dad, divorced from my mom since I was two, had his own up-and-down small business, too, and soon a new wife and kids to take care of. If we had a good year, my mom, my brother, and I moved into a bigger apartment. A bad spell, and I'd notice the mail going unopened in neat but worrisome piles on the hall table. I now know we were in what economists call the fragile middle class, all income from volatile earnings and no inherited wealth or assets to fall back on. We were the kind of middle class in the kind of community that kept us a stone's throw from real poverty, and I think this shaped the way I see the world. My mother took us with her to work in Chicago's notorious Robert Taylor public housing projects while she gave health lessons to young mothers, and some of my earliest playmates were kids with disabilities in a group home where she also worked. (It seemed she was always working.) We had cousins and neighbors who had more than we did, and some who had far less, but we never learned to peg that to their worth. It just wasn't part of our story.

I did learn, though, to ask "why," undoubtedly to an annoying degree. In the backseat of the station wagon facing the rear window, I asked why there were so many people sleeping on the grates on Lower Wacker Drive downtown, huddled together in that odd, un-sunny yellow lamplight. Why did the big plant over on Kedzie have to close, and would another one open and hire everybody back? Why was Ralph's family's furniture out on the curb, and where did their landlord think Ralph was going to live now?

My father turned eighteen the year the Voting Rights Act was signed, 1965; my mother did when the Fair Housing Act was signed three years later. That meant that my parents were in the first gen-eration of black Americans to live full adult lives with explicitly racist barriers lowered enough for them even to glimpse the so-called American Dream. And just as they did, the economic rules changed to dim the lights on it, for everyone. In the mid-1960s, the American Dream was as easy to achieve as it ever was or has been since, with good union jobs, low-cost homeownership, strong financial protections, a high minimum wage, and a high tax rate that funded American research, infrastructure, and education. But in the following decades, rapid changes to tax, labor, and trade laws meant that an economy that used to look like a football, fat-ter in the middle, was shaped like a bow tie by my own eighteenth birthday, with a narrow middle class and bulging ends of high- and low-income households.

This is the Inequality Era. Even in the supposedly good economic times before the COVID-19 pandemic that began in 2020, 40 percent of adults were not paid enough to reliably meet their needs for housing, food, health care, and utilities. Only about two out of three workers had jobs with basic benefits: health insurance, a retirement account (even one they had to fund themselves), and paid time off for illness or caregiving. Upward mobility, the very essence of the American idea, has become stagnant, and many of our global competitors are now performing far better on what we have long considered to be the American Dream. On the other end, money is still being made: the 350 biggest corporations pay their CEOs 278 times what they pay their average workers, up from a 58-to-1 ratio in 1989, and nearly two dozen companies have CEO-to-worker pay gaps of over 1,000 to 1. The richest 1 percent own as much wealth as the entire middle class.

I learned how to track these numbers in my early days working at Demos, a research and advocacy think tank working on public policy solutions to inequality, but what I was still asking when I decided to leave it fifteen years later was: Why? Why was there a constituency at all for policies that would make it harder for more people to have a decent life? And why did so many people seem to blame the last folks in line for the American Dream—black and brown people and new immigrants who had just been let in when it became harder to reach—for economic decisions they had no power to influence? When I came across a study by two Boston-based scholars, titled "Whites See Racism as a Zero-Sum Game That They Are Now Losing," something clicked. In a zero-sum game, when one team scores a point, the other loses a point. In a zero-sum society, there's no mutual progress: what's good for one part of the society is bad for others. I decided to pay the study authors a visit.

It was a hot late-summer day when I walked into the inner courtyard at Harvard Business School to meet with Michael Norton and Samuel Sommers, two tall and lean professors of business and psychology, respectively. Harvard Business School is where some of the wealthiest people in America cemented their pedigrees and became indoctrinated in today's winner-take-all version of capitalism. It is an overwhelmingly white club, admittance to which all but guarantees admittance to all other elite clubs. Nonetheless, that's where we sat as these two academics explained to me how, according to the people they'd surveyed, whites were now the subjugated race in America.

Norton and Sommers had begun their research during the first Obama administration, when a white Tea Party movement drove a backlash against the first black president's policy agenda. They had been interested in why so many white Americans felt they were getting left behind, despite the reality of continued white dominance in US life, from corporations to government. (Notwithstanding the black president, 90 percent of state, local, and federal elected officials were white in the mid-2010s.) What Norton and Sommers found in their research grabbed headlines: the white survey respondents rated antiwhite bias as more prevalent in society than anti-black bias. On a scale of 1 to 10, the average white scoring of anti-black bias was 3.6, but whites rated antiwhite bias as a 4.7, and opined that antiwhite bias had accelerated sharply in the mid-1970s.

"We were shocked. It's so contrary to the facts, of course, but here we are, getting calls and emails from white people who saw the headlines and thanked us for revealing the truth about racism in America!" said Norton with a dry laugh.

"It turns out that the average white person views racism as a zero-sum game," added Sommers. "If things are getting better for black people, it must be at the expense of white people."

"But that's not the way black people see it, right?" I asked.

"Exactly. For black respondents, better outcomes for them don't necessarily mean worse outcomes for white people. It's *not* a zero sum," said Norton.

As to why white Americans, who have thirteen times the median household wealth of black Americans, feel threatened by diminished discrimination against black people, neither Sommers nor Norton had an answer that was satisfying to any of us.

"There's not really an explanation," said Professor Sommers.

I needed to find out. I sensed that this core idea that's so resonant with many white Americans—there's an us and a them, and what's good for them is bad for us—was at the root of our country's dysfunction. One might assume that this kind of competitiveness is human nature, but I don't buy it: for one thing, it's more prevalent among white people than other Americans. There is no biological basis for this; there's no causal link between melanin content in one's skin and a zero-sum world view. As it turns out, everything we believe comes from a story we've been told. So I wanted to know, who is telling people this story? Who is selling this story, and how are they profiting from it? If we are ever to reject this zero-sum idea, we'll need first to understand when, and why, it was created. So to begin my journey, I immersed myself in an unvarnished history of our country's birth.

A ZERO-SUM FINANCIAL MODEL

The story of this country's rise from a starving colony to a world superpower is one that can't be told without the central character of race. In the seventeenth century, influential Europeans were starting to create categories of human beings based on skin color, religion, culture, and geography, aiming not just to differentiate but to rank humanity in terms of inherent worth. This hierarchy—backed by pseudoscientists, explorers, and even clergy—gave Europeans moral permission to exploit and enslave. So, from the United States' colonial beginnings, progress for those considered white did come directly at the expense of people considered nonwhite. The US economy depended on systems of exploitation—on literally taking land and labor from racialized others to enrich white colonizers and slaveholders. This made it easy for the powerful to sell the idea that the inverse was also true: that liberation or justice for people of color would necessarily require taking something away from white people.

European invaders of the New World believed that war was the only sure way to separate Indigenous people from the lands they coveted. Their version of settler colonialism set up a zero-sum competition for land that would shape the American economy to the present day, at an unforgivable cost. The death toll of South and North American Indigenous people in the century after first contact was so massive—an estimated 56 million lives, or 90 percent of all the lands' original inhabitants, through either war or disease—that it changed the amount of carbon in the atmosphere.

Such atrocities needed justification. The European invaders and their descendants used religious prejudices: the natives were incurable heathens and incompatible with the civilized peoples of Europe. Another stereotype that served the European profit motive was that Indigenous people wasted their land, so it would be better off if cultivated by productive settlers. Whatever form these rationales took, colonizers shaped their racist ideologies to fit the bill. The motive was greed; cultivated hatred followed. The result was a near genocide that laid waste to rich native cultures in order to fill European treasuries, particularly in Portugal, Spain, and England—and this later fed the individual wealth of white Americans who received the ill-gotten land for free.

Colonial slavery set up a zero-sum relationship between master and enslaved as well. The formula for profit is revenue minus costs, and American colonial slaveholders happened upon the world's most winning version of the formula to date. Land was cheap to free in the colonies, and although the initial cost of buying a captured African person was high, the lifetime of labor, of course, was free.

All the original thirteen colonies had slavery, and slavery legally persisted in the North all the way up to 1846, the year that New Jersey passed a formal emancipation law. The slave economy truly was national in the decades before the Civil War. Wealth wrung from black hands launched the fortunes of Northeastern port cities in Rhode Island; filled the Massachusetts textile mills with cotton; and capitalized the future Wall Street banks through loans that accepted enslaved people as collateral. In 1860, the four million human beings in the domestic slave trade had a market value of $3 billion. In fact, by the time war loomed, New York merchants had gotten so rich from the slave economy—40 percent of the city's exporting businesses through warehousing, shipping insurance, and sales were Southern cotton exports—that the mayor of New York advocated that his city secede along with the South.

In stark and quantifiable terms, the exploitation, enslavement, and murder of African and Indigenous American people created wealth for the white power structure. The elites who profited made no room for the oppressed to share in the rewards from their lands or labor; what others had, they took. The racial zero sum was crafted in the cradle of the New World.

A ZERO-SUM MENTAL MODEL

The colonists in America created their concept of freedom largely by defining it against the bondage of the Africans among them. In the early colonial years, most European new-comers were people at the bottom of the social hierarchy back home, sent to these shores as servants from orphanages, debt-ors' prisons, or poorhouses. Even those born in America had little of what we currently conceive of as freedom: to choose their own work and education or to move at will. But as the threat of cross-racial servant uprisings became real in the late 1600s—particularly after the bloody Bacon's Rebellion, in which a black and white rebel army burned the capital of colonial Vir-ginia to the ground—colonial governments began to separate the servant class based on skin color.

A look through the colonial laws of the 1680s and early 1700s reveals a deliberate effort to legislate a new hierarchy dividing poor whites and the "basically uncivil, unchristian, and above all, unwhite Native and African laborers." Many of the laws oppress-ing workers of color did so to the direct benefit of poor whites, creating a zero-sum relationship between these two parts of the colonial underclass. In 1705, a new Virginia law granted title and protection to the little property that any white servant might have accumulated—and simultaneously confiscated the personal prop-erty of all the enslaved people in the colony. The zero sum was made quite literal when, by the same law, the church in each par-ish sold the slaves' confiscated property and gave the "profits to the poor of the parish," by which they meant, of course, the white poor.

Most Euro-Americans were not, and would likely never be, the wealthy aristocrats who had every social and economic privilege in Europe. Eternal slavery provided a new caste that even the poorest white-skinned person could hover above and define himself against. Just imagine the psychic benefit of being elevated from the bottom of a rigid class hierarchy to a higher place in a new racial hierarchy by dint of something as immutable as your skin color. You can imagine how, whether or not you owned slaves yourself, you might willingly buy into a zero-sum model to gain the sense of freedom that rises with the subordination of others.

For the common white American, the presence of blackness—imagined as naturally enslaved, with no agency or reason, denied each and every one of the enumerated freedoms—gave daily shape to the confines of a new identity just taking shape at the end of the eighteenth century: white, free, citizen. It was as if they couldn't imagine a world where nobody escaped the tyranny they had known in the Old World; if it could be blacks, it wouldn't have to be whites.

AN ENDURING ZERO-SUM STORY

With each generation, the specter of the founding zero sum has found its way back into the American story. It's hard for me to stand here as a descendant of enslaved people and say that the zero sum wasn't true, that the economic impoverishment of people of color did not benefit white people. But I have to remind myself that it was true only in the sense that it is what happened—it didn't have to happen that way. It would have been better for the sum of us if we'd had a different model. Yes, the zero-sum story of racial hierarchy was born along with the country, but it is an invention of the worst elements of our society: people who gained power through ruthless exploitation and kept it by sowing constant division. It has always optimally benefited only the few while limiting the potential of the rest of us, and therefore the whole.

In decade after decade, threats of job competition—between men and women, immigrants and native born, black and white—have perennially revived the fear of loss at another's gain. The people setting up the competition and spreading these fears were never the needy job seekers, but the elite. (Consider the *New York Herald*'s publishing tycoon, James Gordon Bennett Sr., who warned the city's white working classes during the 1860 election that "if Lincoln is elected, you will have to compete with the labor of four million emancipated negroes.") The zero sum is a story sold by wealthy interests for their own profit, and its persistence requires people desperate enough to buy it.

Today, the racial zero-sum story is resurgent because there is a political movement invested in ginning up white resentment toward lateral scapegoats (similarly or worse-situated people of color) to escape accountability for a massive redistribution of wealth from the many to the few. This divide-and-conquer strategy has been essential to the creation and maintenance of the Inequality Era's other most defining feature: the hollowing out of the goods we share.

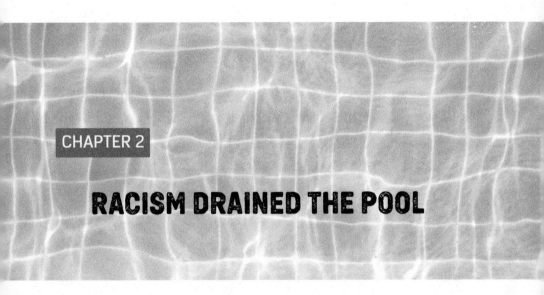

CHAPTER 2

RACISM DRAINED THE POOL

THE UNITED STATES OF AMERICA HAS HAD THE WORLD'S largest economy for most of our history, with enough money to feed and educate all our children, build world-leading infrastructure, and generally ensure a high standard of living for everyone. But we don't. In 2017, our roads, bridges, and water systems got a D+ from the American Society of Civil Engineers. With the exception of about forty years from the New Deal to the 1970s, the United States has had a weaker commitment to public goods, and to the public good, than every country that possesses anywhere near our wealth.

Observers have tried to fit multiple theories onto why Americans are so singularly stingy toward ourselves: Is it a libertarian ideology? The ethos of the Western frontier? Our founding rebellion against government? When I first started working at Demos in my early twenties, the organization had a project called Public Works that tried to understand antigovernment sentiment and find ways of communicating that would overcome it. Community-based advocates who were fighting for things like food stamps, public transit, and education funding sought the project's help as they faced resistance both in their legislatures and when knocking on doors. Public Works' research revealed that people have fuzzy ideas about government, not understanding, for example, that highways, libraries, and public schools are, in fact, government.

As I sat in Demos's staff meeting listening to the two people leading the project present their research, I took notes and nodded. I was just an entry-level staff person not involved in the project, but when the presentation wrapped, I raised my hand. The two presenters were white, liberal advocates from Texas who had spent their lives pushing for economic fairness and opportunity for children. I had no research experience in communications, but having grown up in the 1980s and '90s, I had the impression that every time anybody in politics complained about government programs, they invoked, explicitly or otherwise, lazy black people who were too reliant on government. So, I had to ask, "Did race ever come up in your research?" It turned out they hadn't even asked the question.

Demos eventually stopped working on the Public Works project. Years later, when I set out on my journey to find the roots of our country's dysfunction, I had a chance to come at the question again—but this time, informed by conversations with community organizers, social scientists, politicians, and historians who did ask the question, I was able to discover a more convincing rationale for why so many Americans had such a dim view of government.

AN UNLIKELY ABOLITIONIST

In 1857, a white Southerner named Hinton Rowan Helper published a book called *The Impending Crisis of the South: How to Meet It*. Helper had taken it upon himself to count how many schools, libraries, and other public institutions had been set up in free states compared to slave states. In Pennsylvania, for instance, he counted 393 libraries; in South Carolina, just 26. In Maine, 236; in Georgia, 38. New Hampshire had 2,381 public schools; Mississippi 782. The disparity was similar everywhere he looked.

Helper was an avowed racist, and yet he railed against slavery because he saw what it was doing to his fellow white Southerners. The slave economy was a system that created high concentrations of wealth, land, and political power. "Notwithstanding the fact that the white non-slaveholders of the South are in the majority, as five to one, they have never yet had any part or lot in framing the laws under which they live," Helper wrote. And without a voice in the policy-making, common white Southerners were unable to win much for themselves. In a way, the plantation class made an understandable calculation: a governing class will tax themselves to invest in amenities that serve the public (schools, libraries, roads and utilities, support for local businesses) because they need to. The wealthy need these assets in a community to make it livable for them, but also, more importantly, to attract and retain the people on whom their profits depend, be they workers or customers.

For the owners in the slave economy, however, neither was strictly necessary. The primary source of plantation wealth was a completely captive and unpaid labor force. Owners didn't need more than a handful of white workers per plantation. They didn't need an educated populace, whether black or white; such a thing was in fact counter to their financial interest. And their farms didn't depend on many local customers, whether individuals or businesses: the market for cotton was a global exchange, and the factories that bought their raw goods were in the North, staffed by wage laborers. Life on a plantation was self-contained; the welfare of the surrounding community mattered little outside the closed system.

With his book, Hinton Rowan Helper aimed to destroy that system. He even took on the most common objection to abolition at the time: the question of how to compensate slave owners for their losses (which President Lincoln managed for District of Columbia slave owners loyal to the Union during the Civil War, at $300 per enslaved person). But Helper argued that owners should actually have to compensate the rest of the white citizens of the South, because slavery had impoverished the region. The value of Northern land was more than five times the value of Southern land per acre, he calculated, despite the South's advantage in climate, minerals, and soil. Because the Southern "oligarchs of the lash," as he called them, had done so little to support education, innovation, and small enterprise, slavery was making Southern whites poorer.

Today, according to the US Census Bureau, nine of the ten poorest states in the nation are in the South. So are seven of the ten states with the least educational attainment. In 2007, economist Nathan Nunn, a soft-spoken Harvard professor then in his midthirties, made waves with a piece of research showing the reach of slavery into the modern Southern economy. Nunn found that the well-known story of deprivation in the American South was not uniform and, in fact, followed a historical logic: counties that relied more on slave labor in 1860 had lower per capita incomes in 2000.

Nunn's research showed that although of course slave counties had higher inequality during the era of slavery (particularly of land), it wasn't the degree of inequality that was correlated with poverty today; it was the fact of slavery itself, whether on large plantations or small farms. When I talked to Nathan Nunn, he couldn't say exactly how the hand of slavery was strangling opportunity generations later. He made it clear, however, that it wasn't just the black inhabitants who were faring worse today; it was the white families in the counties, too. When slavery was abolished, Confederate states found themselves far behind Northern states in the creation of the public infrastructure that supports economic mobility, and they continue to lag behind today. These deficits limit economic mobility for all residents, not just the descendants of enslaved people.

THE POWER OF PUBLIC GOODS

A functioning society rests on a web of mutuality, a willingness among all involved to share enough with one another to accomplish what no one person can do alone. In a sense, that's what government is. I can't create my own electric grid, school system, internet, or health care system—and the most efficient way to ensure that those things are created and available to all on a fair and open basis is to fund and provide them publicly. If you want the quality and availability of those things to vary based on how much money an individual has, you may argue for privatization—but even advocates of privatization still want the government, not corporations, to shoulder the investment cost for massive infrastructure needs. For most of the twentieth century, leaders of both parties agreed on the wisdom of those investments, from Democratic president Franklin D. Roosevelt's Depression-era jobs programs to Republican president Eisenhower's Interstate Highway System to Republican Richard Nixon's Supplemental Security Income for the elderly and people with disabilities.

Yet almost every clause of the American social contract had an asterisk. For most of our history, the beneficiaries of America's free public investments were whites only. The list of free stuff? It's long. The Homestead Act of 1862 offered 160 acres of expropriated Indigenous land west of the Mississippi to any citizen or person eligible for citizenship (which, after the 1790 Naturalization Act, was only white immigrants) if they could reach the land and build on it. A free grant of property! Fewer than six thousand black families were able to become part of the 1.6 million landowners who gained deeds through the Homestead Act and its 1866 Southern counterpart. Today, an estimated 46 million people are propertied descendants of Homestead Act beneficiaries.

During the Great Depression, the American government told banks it would insure mortgages on real estate if they made them longer-term and more affordable (offering tax deductions on interest along the way)—but the government drew red "Do Not Lend" lines (known as redlining) around almost all the black neighborhoods in the country with a never-substantiated assumption that they would be bad credit risks.

The New Deal transformed the lives of workers with minimum wage and overtime laws—but compromises with Southern Democrats excluded the job categories most black people held, in domestic and agricultural work. Then the GI Bill of 1944 paid the college tuition of hundreds of thousands of veterans, catapulting a generation of men into professional careers—but few black veterans benefited, as local administrators funneled most black servicemen to segregated vocational schools. The mortgage benefit in the GI Bill pushed the postwar white homeownership rate to three out of four white families—but with federally sanctioned housing discrimination, the black and Latinx rates stayed at around two out of five, despite the attempts of veterans of color to participate.

The federal government created suburbs by investing in the federal highway system and subsidizing private housing developers—but demanded racial covenants ("whites only" clauses in housing contracts) to prevent black people from buying into them. Social Security gave income to millions of elderly Americans—but again, exclusions of job categories left most black workers out, and Southern congresspeople opposed more generous cash aid for the elderly poor. You could even consider the New Deal labor laws that encouraged collective bargaining to be a no-cost government subsidy to create a white middle class, as many unions kept their doors closed to nonwhites until the 1960s.

Between the era of the New Deal and the civil rights movement, these and more government policies worked to ensure a large, secure, and white middle class. But once desegregation lowered barriers, people with power (politicians and executives, but also individual white homeowners, business owners, shop stewards, and community leaders) faced the possibility of sharing those benefits. The advantages white people had accumulated were free and usually invisible, and so conferred an elevated status that seemed natural and almost innate. White society had repeatedly denied people of color economic benefits on the premise that they were inferior; those unequal benefits then reinforced the hierarchy, making whites actually economically superior. What would it mean to white people, both materially and psychologically, if the supposedly inferior people received the same treatment from the government? The period since integration has tested many whites' commitment to the public, in ways big and small.

THE SWIMMING POOLS

The American landscape was once graced with resplendent public swimming pools, some big enough to hold thousands of swimmers at a time. In the 1920s, towns and cities tried to outdo one another by building the most elaborate pools; in the 1930s, the Works Progress Administration put people to work building hundreds more. By World War II, the country's two thousand pools were glittering symbols of a new commitment by local officials to the quality of life of their residents, allowing hundreds of thousands of people to socialize together for free. A particular social agenda undergirded these public investments. Officials envisioned the distinctly American phenomenon of the grand public resort pools as "social melting pots." Like free public grade schools, public pools were part of an "Americanizing" project intended to overcome ethnic divisions and cohere a common identity—and it worked. A Pennsylvania county recreation director said, "Let's build bigger, better and finer pools. That's real democracy. Take away the sham and hypocrisy of clothes, don a swimsuit, and we're all the same." Of course, that vision of classlessness wasn't expansive enough to include skin color that wasn't, in fact, "all the same." By the 1950s, the fight to integrate America's prized public swimming pools would demonstrate the limits of white support for public goods.

In 1953, a thirteen-year-old black boy named Tommy Cummings drowned in Baltimore's Patapsco River while swimming with three friends, two white and one black. The friends had been forced to swim in the dangerous waterway because none of the city's seven public pools allowed interracial swimming. Tommy was one of three black children to die that summer in open water, and civil rights advocates sued the city. They won on appeal three years later, and on June 23, 1956, for the first time, all Baltimore children had the chance to swim with other children, regardless of skin color. Public recreation free from discrimination could, in the minds of the city's progressive community, foster more friendships like the one Tommy was trying to enjoy when he drowned. What ended up happening, however, was not the promised mingling of children of different races. In Baltimore, instead of sharing the pool, white children stopped going to the pools that black children could easily access, and white adults informally policed (through intimidation and violence) the public pools in white neighborhoods.

In America's smaller towns, where there was only one public pool, desegregation called into question what "public" really meant. Black community members pressed for access to the public resource that their tax dollars had helped to build. If assets were public, they argued, they must be furnished on an equal basis. Instead, white public officials took the public assets private, creating new private corporations to run the pools. The town of Warren, Ohio, dealt with its integration problem by creating the members-only Veterans' Swim Club, which selected members based on a secret vote. (The club promptly selected only white residents of the town.) The small coal town of Montgomery, West Virginia, built a new resort pool in 1942 but let it lay untouched for four years while black residents argued that the state's civil rights law required equal access. Unable to tolerate the idea of sharing the pool with black people, city leaders eventually formed a private "Park Association" whose sole job was to administer the pool, and the city leased the public asset to the private association for $1. Only white residents were allowed admission. Warren and Montgomery were just two of countless towns—in every region in America, not just the South—where the fight over public pools revealed that for many white Americans, the word *public* did not mean "of the people." It meant "of the white people." They replaced the assets of a community with the privileges of a club.

Eventually, the exclusion boomeranged on white citizens. In Montgomery, Alabama, the Oak Park pool was the grandest one for miles, the crown jewel of a Parks Department that also included a zoo, a community center, and a dozen other public parks. Of course, the pool was for whites only; the entire public parks system was segregated. Dorothy Moore was a white teenage lifeguard when a federal court deemed the town's segregated recreation unconstitutional. Suddenly, black children would be able to wade into the deep end with white children at the Oak Park pool; at the rec center, black elders would get chairs at the card tables. The reaction of the city council was swift—effective January 1, 1959, the Parks Department would be no more.

The council decided to drain the pool rather than share it with their black neighbors. Of course, the decision meant that white families lost a public resource as well. "It was miserable," Mrs. Moore told a reporter five decades later. Uncomprehending white children cried as the city contractors poured dirt into the pool, paved it over, and seeded it with grass that was green by the time summer came along again. To defy desegregation, Montgomery would go on to close every single public park and padlock the doors of the community center. It even sold off the animals in the zoo. The entire public park system would stay closed for over a decade. Even after it reopened, they never rebuilt the pool.

The loss of the Oak Park pool was replicated across the country. Instead of complying with a desegregation order, New Orleans closed what was known as the largest pool in the South, Audubon Pool, in 1962, for seven years. In Winona, Mississippi, if you know where to look, you can still see the metal railings of the old pool's diving board amid overgrown weeds; in nearby Stonewall, a real estate developer unearthed the carcass of the segregated pool in the mid-2000s. Even in towns that didn't immediately drain their public pools, integration ended the public pool's glory years, as white residents abandoned the pools en masse.

Built in 1919, the Fairground Park pool in St. Louis, Missouri, was the largest in the country and probably the world, with a sandy beach, an elaborate diving board, and a reported capacity of ten thousand swimmers. When a new city administration changed the parks policy in 1949 to allow black swimmers, the first integrated swim ended in bloodshed. On June 21, two hundred white residents surrounded the pool with "bats, clubs, bricks and knives" to menace the first thirty or so black swimmers. Over the course of the day, a white mob that grew to five thousand attacked every black person in sight around the Fairground Park. After the Fairground Park Riot, as it was known, the city returned to a segregation policy using public safety as a justification, but a successful NAACP lawsuit reopened the pool to all St. Louisans the following summer. On the first day of integrated swimming, July 19, 1950, only seven white swimmers attended, joining three brave black swimmers under the shouts of two hundred white protestors. That first integrated summer, Fairground logged just 10,000 swims—down from 313,000 the previous summer. The city closed the pool for good six years later. Racial hatred led to St. Louis draining one of the most prized public pools in the world.

Draining public swimming pools to avoid integration received the official blessing of the US Supreme Court in 1971. The city council in Jackson, Mississippi, had responded to desegregation demands by closing four public pools and leasing the fifth to the YMCA, which operated it for whites only. Black citizens sued, but the Supreme Court, in *Palmer v. Thompson*, held that a city could choose not to provide a public facility rather than maintain an integrated one, because by robbing the entire public, the white leaders were spreading equal harm. "There was no evidence of state action affecting Negroes differently from white," wrote Justice Hugo Black. The court went on to turn a blind eye to the obvious racial animus behind the decision, taking the race neutrality at face value. The decision showed the limits of the civil rights legal tool kit and forecast the politics of public services for decades to come: If the benefits can't be whites-only, you can't have them at all. And if you say it's racist? Well, prove it.

As Jeff Wiltse writes in his history of pool desegregation, *Contested Waters: A Social History of Swimming Pools in America*, "Beginning in the mid-1950s northern cities generally stopped building large resort pools and let the ones already constructed fall into disrepair." Over the next decade, millions of white Americans who once swam in public for free began to pay rather than swim for free with black people; desegregation in the midfifties coincided with a surge in backyard pools and members-only swim clubs. In Washington, DC, for example, 125 new private swim clubs were opened in less than a decade following pool desegregation in 1953. The classless utopia faded, replaced by clubs with $200 membership fees and annual dues. A once-public resource became a luxury amenity, and entire communities lost out on the benefits of public life and civic engagement once understood to be the key to making American democracy real.

Today, we don't even notice the absence of the grand resort pools in our communities; where grass grows over former sites, there are no plaques to tell the story of how racism drained the pools. But the spirit that drained these public goods lives on. The impulse to exclude now manifests in a subtler fashion, more often reflected in a pool of resources than a literal one.

CHAPTER 3

GOING WITHOUT

FOR GENERATIONS, COLLEGE-GOING WHITE AMERICANS could count on public money from their governments, whether federal or state, to pay most if not all of the costs of higher education. The idea of flourishing public colleges—at least one in every state—took shape in the 1860s, when the US government offered the states over ten million acres of land taken from Indigenous people to build on or to sell for institutions of higher education for their citizens. More free federal money for higher education came with the GI Bill, which paid tuition plus living expenses for World War II veterans and swelled college coffers: in 1947, veterans made up 50 percent of US college admissions. (Racist program administration and educational segregation left black veterans in the South largely excluded from these opportunities, however.) Public commitment to college for all was a crucial part of the white social contract for much of the twentieth century. In 1976, state governments provided $6 out of every $10 of the cost of students attending public colleges. The remainder translated into modest tuition bills—just $617 at a four-year college in 1976, and a student could receive a federal Pell Grant for as much as $1,400 against that and living expenses. Many of the country's biggest and most respected public colleges were tuition-free, from the City University of New York to the University of California system. This massive public investment wasn't considered charity; an individual state saw a return of $3 to $4 for every $1 it invested in public colleges. When *the public* meant "white," public colleges thrived.

That's no longer the case. Students of color made up just one in six public college students in 1980, but they now make up over four in ten. Over this period of growth among students of color, ensuring college affordability fell out of favor with lawmakers. State legislatures began to drastically cut what they spent per student on their public colleges, even as the taxable income base in the state grew. More and more Americans enrolled nonetheless, because other policy decisions in the labor market made a college degree necessary to compete for a middle-class job. By 2017, the majority of state colleges were relying on student tuition dollars for the majority of their expenses. The average public college tuition has nearly tripled since 1991, helping bring its counterpart, skyrocketing student debt, to $1.5 trillion in 2020.

The rising cost of college feels to most Americans like so many aspects of our economy: unexplained and unavoidable. But at Demos, we researched the causes of rising tuition and linked them squarely to the withering government commitment to public funding. The federal government for its part slowly shifted its financial aid from grants that didn't have to be repaid (such as Pell Grants for low-income students, which used to cover four-fifths of college costs and now cover at most one-third) to federal loans, which, if we're honest, are not financial aid at all. Yes, student loans enable Americans to pay their college bills during enrollment, but the compounding interest means they must pay at least 33 percent more on average than the amount borrowed. Millions of students are also paying double-digit interest on private loans.

The new "debt-for-diploma system," as my former Demos colleague Tamara Draut called it, has impacted black students most acutely, as generations of racist policies have left our families with less wealth to draw on to pay for college. Eight out of ten black graduates have to borrow, and at higher levels than any other group. In my high school, the seniors had a tradition of posting college admissions letters on the school counselor's wall: right side up for acceptance, sideways for waitlist, and upside down for rejection. So much bravado in that transparency, and yet nobody was putting their financial aid letters on the wall. I borrowed five figures for college and nearly six for law school, including a high-interest private loan that my grandmother had to cosign. At forty years old, I'm still paying it all off, and I don't know a single black peer who's not in the same boat, even those whose parents were doctors and lawyers. Because wealth is largely shaped by how much money your parents and grandparents had, black young adults' efforts at higher education and higher earnings aren't putting much of a dent in the racial wealth gap. This generation was born too late for the free ride, and student loan repayment is making it even harder for black graduates' savings and assets to catch up. In fact, white high school dropouts have higher average household wealth than black people who've graduated from college.

As with so many economic ills, student debt is most acute among black families, but it has now reached 63 percent of white public college graduates as well and is having ripple effects across our entire economy. In 2019, the Federal Reserve reported on what most of my generation knows: student debt payments are stopping us from buying our first home, the irreplaceable wealth-building asset. Debt is even contributing to delays in marriage and family formation. And by age thirty, young adults with debt have half the retirement savings of those who are debt-free.

Fundamentally, we have to ask ourselves, how was it fair and how was it smart to price a degree out of reach for the working class just as that degree became the price of entry into the middle class? And how is it fair or smart to create a new source of debt for a generation when that debt makes it harder for us to achieve the hallmarks of middle-class security: a house, marriage, and retirement savings? There is neither fairness nor wisdom in this system, only self-sabotage. Other countries learned from the midcentury American investment in higher education and have now raced ahead. A third of developed countries offer free tuition, and another third keep tuition lower than $2,600. In the United States, recent policy proposals to restore free college are generally popular, though race shapes public opinion. There's a 30-percentage-point gap in support for free college between white people on the one hand (53 percent) and black and Latinx Americans on the other

(86 and 82 percent). The most fiercely opposed? Among the very people who benefited the most from the largely whites-only free college model and who now want to pull the ladder up behind them: older, college-educated (white) Republicans.

In the story of how America drained the pool of our public college system, racism is the uncredited actor.

FUNDING JAILS, NOT BOOKS

The rise in student diversity shifted the politics of state education spending across the country. As part of the antigovernment fervor in the 1980s and '90s, spending on the well-being of youth fell out of favor, but meanwhile, legislatures were tripling their expenditures on incarceration and policing. By 2016, eighteen states were spending more on jails and prisons than they were on colleges and universities. The path to this system of mass incarceration is another story of racist policy-making creating unsustainable costs for everyone.

The loss of good factory jobs in the mid-1970s hit the cities first, and with cities, their segregated black residents. Instead of responding to the economic problem with economic development, jobs programs, and stronger safety nets, the federal government cut back massively on urban social spending in the 1980s. In its place, it waged a drug war. Dehumanizing and unpitying stereotypes about the dangers of drug use in the inner cities fueled a new era of harsher sentencing and post-release penalties to create a system of mass incarceration. While the so-called crack epidemic is far behind us, the system rolls on, and today, more than 1.25 million people are arrested each year for drug possession. These are not kingpins or high-level dealers; more than four times as many people are arrested for possessing drugs as for selling drugs, often in amounts so tiny they can only be intended for personal use. In 2016, the number of arrests for marijuana possession exceeded the total number of arrests for all violent crimes put together.

The racist nature of our mass incarceration system has been well documented. White and black people are equally likely to use drugs, but the system is six times as likely to incarcerate black people for a drug crime. Sentences for possession of crack cocaine, which is more widely used by African Americans than whites, are about eighteen times harsher than penalties for the powder version of the drug, which is used more often by whites. For decades before policy changes in 2010, this sentencing disparity was about one hundred to one.

Over the last twenty years, however, a striking change has taken place. Getting locked up over drugs and related property crimes has become more and more common among white people and less so among black folks. A primary factor in this shift is, as the *New York Times* wrote, the fact that "Mostly white and politically conservative counties have continued to send more drug offenders to prison, reflecting the changing geography of addiction. While crack cocaine addiction was centered in cities, opioid and meth addiction are ravaging small communities" in largely white locales. The "pathology" long ascribed to urban communities as integral and immutable characteristics of black life (drug addiction, property crimes to support a habit, broken families) has now moved, with deindustrialization, into the suburbs and the countryside. By 2018, an estimated 130 people were dying every day from opioid overdoses, and over ten million people were abusing prescription opioids.

The option to treat poverty and drug addiction as a public health and economic security issue rather than a criminal one has always been present. Will our nation choose that option now that white people, always the majority of drug users, make up a soaring population of people for whom addiction takes over? The woes that devastated communities of color are now visiting white America, and the costs of incarceration are coming due in suburban and rural areas, squeezing state budgets and competing with education. It's not a comeuppance but a bitter cost of the white majority's willingness to accept the suffering of others, a cost of racism itself.

ISSUES OF EDUCATION

As racialized as the politics of government spending has become, the victims of the new higher education austerity include the majority of white students. When Demos was working to build the research case for debt-free college, we partnered with a then-small online group organizing students and graduates with debt, called the Student Debt Crisis Center. Now more than one million members strong, the Student Debt Crisis Center—run by Natalia Abrams, a white Millennial grad of the University of California,

Los Angeles—speaks for an indebted generation, lifting up the stories it collects in an online story bank. "We recently polled the activists on our list, and about seventy percent identify as white," Abrams told me.

Josh Frost is thirty-nine and works full-time at a news station and part-time at a gas station. He pays three-quarters of his salary toward his student debt while living with his parents. Though he did everything society told him to do, he's nearing forty but feels like adulthood is passing him by: "I'm watching everyone I know start families and buy homes," he said. Emilie Scott needed to go to college to fulfill her goal of becoming a teacher. She worked four jobs while studying, to keep her borrowing low, but still graduated with $70,000 in private and public student loans. Four years after graduation, making payments of $600 a month, she has paid off $28,000, but because of interest rates close to 10 percent, her remaining balance is $65,000. "This is madness," she says. "How can I keep up with this? And for how long?" Unfortunately for Emilie, more than three million senior citizens who still owe $86 billion in student loans can attest that the "madness" doesn't really end. Seniors with student loans are more likely to report rationing medical care, and the government garnishes Social Security payments for seniors in default.

Robert Settle Jr. was sixty years old in 2016, and although he is completely disabled and lost all his savings in the financial crisis of 2008, he is still being sued for $60,000 in private student loans he obtained while working for a master's degree to advance his career.

Robert points his ire at the government for allowing this system to flourish, and he is eager to tell his story. "I want the entire country to see how a disabled, elderly couple is treated by our federal government!"

The flourishing of a society can in large part be measured by the education of its people. College attainment isn't just beneficial for individuals; it's vital for our democracy. Now more than ever, we must refill the pool of public resources to liberate a generation from burdensome student debt and restore the system of debt-free public college for all.

COSTING OUR HEALTH

The sudden demise of our public college system and the growing scourge of student debt are recent phenomena, but there may be no question that has vexed Americans for longer than why our health care system isn't better: more affordable, less complex, more secure for everyone. We pay more individually and as a nation for health care and have worse health outcomes than our industrialized peers, all of whom have some version of publicly financed universal coverage. But the United States doesn't—even though the closest thing we have to European-style single-payer care, Medicare for the elderly, is successful economically and popular with its beneficiaries. (Even the theoretical opposition to universal health care is weaker than it seems; at the height of public opposition to the Affordable Care Act, eleven out of twelve of the bill's core ideas polled with majority support.) In the modern era, more elections have been won, lost, and fought on health care than on any other single issue besides the overall economy. Why can't we fix this?

In some ways, the story of America's health care dysfunction comes back to the pool. Health insurers use that exact term when they refer to the number of people in the "risk pool" of a plan. A high number minimizes the risk posed by any individual's health costs. Whether we're talking about insurance or drug trials or vaccines or improvements to medical practice, in health, the key is getting everybody in. Health care works best as a collective endeavor, and that's at the heart of why America's system performs so poorly. We've resisted universal solutions because when it comes to health care, from President Truman's first national proposal in 1945 to the present-day battles over Medicaid expansion, racism has stopped us from ever filling the pool in the first place.

Senator Claude Pepper of Florida was a towering figure topped with bright red hair. He gained national prominence when he became President Harry Truman's most reliable Southern Democratic champion for national health insurance. According to Jill Quadagno, who tells the story in her book *One Nation, Uninsured,* Claude Pepper was "a farm boy from the red clay country of eastern Alabama who never saw a paved road until he went to college [and] entered public life because he believed that government could be a force to enhance the greater good." That farm boy never would have anticipated he'd grow up to be public enemy number one of the American Medical Association. The AMA is a trade group of doctors known to most Americans now for its labeling on consumer products, but in the 1940s, it acted as a scorched-earth lobbying group whose leadership viewed any kind of insurance that mediated between the patient and the doctor with suspicion. Government insurance, with the potential for cost rationing, portended a threat to the profitability of the entire medical profession. The AMA launched the first modern public relations and lobbying campaign to paint government insurance as a threat not to doctors' finances, however—but to the entire American way of life. They labeled the idea socialist.

After Pepper came out as a champion of government-funded health care and other liberal programs, he became a prime target in the 1950 election. The effort to unseat him was a coordinated campaign by a group of businessmen who "collected every photo of Pepper with African Americans . . . and charged that northern labor bosses were 'paying ten to twenty dollars to blacks to register' and vote for him." The physicians' lobby joined in, running newspaper ads that included a photo of Senator Pepper with Paul Robeson, the black celebrity and Communist activist. The racist red-baiting campaign worked. Universal health care's biggest Senate champion lost his 1950 race by more than sixty thousand votes.

The bare-knuckle assault on universal health insurance signaled the beginning of the end of the New Deal Democrats' reign in national politics. Liberal Southern Democrats who saw the transformative potential in government action, like Claude Pepper, were a dying breed, and Harry Truman could not get the segregationist caucus of Southern "Dixiecrat" Democrats in his party behind his vision of national health care. Truman was the first president to champion civil rights since Reconstruction, desegregating the armed forces and forming a President's Committee on Civil Rights. The Southern Democratic bloc saw the civil rights potential in his health care plan—which was designed to be universal, without racial discrimination—as too great a cost to bear for the benefit of bringing health care to their region. As Jill Quadagno writes, "If national health insurance succeeded, it would be without the support of the South." Needless to say, it would not succeed. Truman declined to run again in 1952, and national health insurance receded from the legislative agenda for the next decade.

To be clear, the beneficiaries of Truman's universal coverage would have been overwhelmingly white, as white people at the time made up 90 percent of the US population. Few Americans, black or white, had private insurance plans, and the recent notion that employers would provide it had yet to solidify into a nationwide expectation. The pool of national health insurance would have been mainly for white Americans, but the threat of sharing it with even a small number of black and brown Americans helped to doom the entire plan from the start.

After the defeat of Truman's proposal, unions increasingly pressed employers for health care benefits for workers and retirees. By the 1960s, as part of his "war on poverty," President Johnson created a generous federal health care program for the elderly (an even whiter population than the overall population) in Medicare and a less generous patchwork for low-income people and children, Medicaid. Johnson's Congress conceded that it would leave whether and how to offer Medicaid to the individual states, in a compromise with racism that curtailed the program's reach for decades. Medicaid was intended to insure all Americans living in poverty by 1970, but by 1985, the Robert Wood Johnson Foundation estimated that less than half of low-income families were covered. Then corporations began cutting back on offering health benefits to their employees in the 1980s, and the number of uninsured skyrocketed. As of 2022 we still have no universal health insurance.

The closest the United States has come to a universal plan is the Affordable Care Act, created by a black president carried into office with record turnout among black voters and passed with no congressional votes from the Republican Party. The Affordable Care Act created state-based markets for consumers to comparison-shop health care plans, with federal subsidies for moderate- to middle-income purchasers. It also stopped private insurance companies from some of their most unpopular practices, such as denying insurance to people with preexisting conditions, dropping customers when they were sick, and requiring young adults to leave their parents' insurance before age twenty-six. But Congress rejected the reform ideas that would have relied the most on Americans swimming in one national pool: a federal "public option" plan and collective bargaining to lower prescription drug costs. The idea of a Truman-style national health insurer never made it to a vote. As comparatively modest as it was, Obamacare has been deeply unpopular with the majority of white voters. White support remained under 40 percent until after the law's namesake left office, and as of this writing, it has yet to surpass the 50 percent mark.

Blame President Obama—not for strategic missteps; blame him for being black. Numerous social science studies have shown that racial resentment among white people spiked with the election of Barack Obama. When the figurehead of American government became a black man in 2009, the correlation between views on race and views on government and policy went into overdrive. Professor Michael Tesler, a political scientist at Brown University, conducted research on the way race and racial attitudes impacted Americans' views of the Affordable Care Act in 2010. He concluded that whites with higher levels of racial resentment and more anti-black stereotypes grew more opposed to health care reform after it became associated with President Obama. "Racial attitudes . . . had a considerably larger impact on our panel respondents' health care opinions in November 2009 than they did before Barack Obama became the Democratic nominee for president," Tesler explained in a Brown University interview. He also ran an experiment to try to disassociate health reform proposals from Obama. "The experiments . . . revealed that health care policies were significantly more racialized when they were framed as part of President Obama's plan than they were for respondents told that these exact same proposals were part of President Clinton's 1993 reform efforts."

THE LOSS OF RURAL HOSPITALS

Rural America is experiencing a quiet crisis. Rural hospitals account for one in seven jobs in their areas, but over the past ten years, 120 rural hospitals have closed, dealing a body blow to the economy and health of the country's mostly white, overwhelmingly conservative rural communities. A quarter of the remaining rural hospitals are at risk of closing. One thing that all of the states with the highest hospital closures have in common is that their legislatures have all refused to expand Medicaid under Obamacare.

Texas leads the country in rural hospital closures, with twenty-six hospitals permanently closing or whittling down services since 2010. The state has half the hospitals it had in the 1960s. In 2013, an eighteen-month-old died after choking on a grape because her parents couldn't reach the nearest hospital in time. The outrage from that story swept the state, but it was short-lived. What would reopen the hospitals, according to Don McBeath, an expert in rural medicine who now does government relations for a Texas network of rural hospitals called TORCH, is something that the powers that be in the state capital are dead set against. That's Medicaid—both fully funding Texas's share and expanding eligibility for it, as Congress intended with the Affordable Care Act.

I caught up with McBeath by phone at the beginning of the COVID-19 outbreak and asked him if, as my research had suggested, Medicaid expansion would help shore up the rural hospital system. "I'm sure you're aware, Texas has probably one of the narrowest Medicaid coverage programs in the country," he said. I was aware. I'd had to double-check the figure because I couldn't believe it was so low, but in fact, if you make as little as $4,000 a year, you're considered too rich to qualify for Medicaid in Texas, and even that has exclusions, as McBeath explained.

"I hear this all the time: even some of my friends will go, 'Oh, those lazy bums. They need to get off that Medicaid and go to work.' And I go, 'Excuse me? Who do you think's on Medicaid?' First of all, there's no men on Medicaid, period, in Texas. No adult men, unless they have a disability and they're poor. And there's no nonpregnant women, I don't care how poor they are."

Failing to insure so many people leaves a lot of unpaid medical bills in the state, and that drains the Texas hospital system. The conservative majority in the Texas legislature has been so opposed to the idea of Medicaid that they shortchange the state's hospitals in compensating for the few (mostly pregnant women) Medicaid patients they see. Then, by rejecting Obamacare's Medicaid expansion, they lose out on federal money that would insure about 1.5 million Texas citizens. As a result of this and some federal policies, including budget cuts in the government sequestration that the Tea Party forced during Obama's second term, rural health care is rapidly disappearing. Texas politicians' government-bashing is both ideological and strategic; they benefit politically by stopping government from having a beneficial presence in people's lives. Then, as white constituents' needs mount, the claim that government is busy serving some racialized other instead of them becomes more convincing.

McBeath sighed. "The thing that we've seen in this state is, our politicians have so demonized the term 'Medicaid expansion' that they'll never reverse course on that as long as they're in control. And we can prove to them all day long that [it] may be the way to go. But . . . we quit barking up that tree, because we're not gonna get anywhere."

What the mostly white and male conservatives in the Texas legislature are doing to sabotage the state's health care system doesn't hurt them personally—the state provides their health insurance—but it's costing their state millions.

Expanding Medicaid should be a no-brainer for states, cost-wise. The federal government paid 120 percent of the cost for the first few years and 90 percent into the future. The states that expanded saw hundreds of thousands of their working-class citizens go from being uninsured—where an accident can cause bankruptcy and preventable illnesses can become fatal—to being able to afford to see a doctor. The benefits don't stop with individual people, though. Stable Medicaid funding has allowed rural medical clinics in expansion states to thrive financially. In Arkansas, the first Southern state to accept expanded Medicaid, a health clinic in one of the poorest towns in the country has constructed a new building, created jobs, and served more patients, causing measurable improvements in the community's health. Terrence Aikens, an outreach employee at the clinic, told a reporter in 2020, "What we've experienced in the last few years has been nothing short of amazing."

Why wouldn't a state's politicians take free money to have such amazing health and economic outcomes in their communities, including rural ones with disproportionate conservative representation and fewer options for economic activity? It's not that it's unpopular; expanding Medicaid has polled higher than Obamacare since the bill passed. The answer is all too familiar: racism. Colleen M. Grogan and Sunggeun (Ethan) Park of the University of Chicago found that racialization affects state Medicaid decision-making. First, they found that just after the 2012 Supreme Court decision that made it optional, Medicaid expansion had robust support among black and Latinx Americans at 82 and 65 percent respectively, but slightly below-majority support among white Americans, at 46 percent. Across the country, state-level support for Medicaid expansion ranged between about 45 and 55 percent, and interestingly, some of the highest support was found in the South (where the larger black populations drove up the average).

But that larger black population also prompted a sense of group threat and backlash from the white power structure; Grogan and Park found "as the percent of the black population increases, the likelihood of adoption decreases." The zero-sum story again. As with the public swimming pools, public health care is often a benefit that white people have little interest in sharing with their black neighbors. Grogan and Park's model found that it didn't matter whether a state's communities of color supported the expansion if the white community, with its greater political power and representation, did not. "State adoption decisions are positively related to white opinion and do not respond to nonwhite support levels," they concluded.

When I pointed out this study to Ginny Goldman, veteran community organizer in Texas, she threw her hands up. For ten years, Ginny built a nonprofit called the Texas Organizing Project (TOP), which aimed to improve Texas's democracy by engaging residents of color in issue activism and elections. Ginny gives one the impression of being battery-powered. She's a fast talker with eyes that size you up quickly—but she's just as quick to reveal her deep compassion for people who struggle. The idea that it wouldn't matter how much black and brown Texas supported better health care if white Texas did not—"it just flies in the face of everything that we spend our time doing," she told me. Ginny tells her members, "There's power in numbers. You're the majority. You have to organize. You've got to get out. You've got to vote. You've got to be loud!" But then, as the study I showed her suggested, "there's actually this tiny sliver of a minority of people who will outdo you."

I asked Ginny what arguments Texas's leaders made for turning away free money to help solve that state's worst-in-the-nation health coverage crisis. She recalled accompanying TOP members to state legislative hearings, "and Republican legislators would say, you know, 'These folks are gonna come out of the woodwork like bugs.' These freeloaders who are just gonna come out from everywhere. And comparing them to insects and bugs . . . rodents. Asking for stuff."

This particular racist trope, the language of infestation, is usually deployed against immigrants and, in the current immigration debates, those from Latin America. In Texas, Latinx people are the largest group of uninsured. But Ginny saw how some in the very community that would be most helped by Medicaid expansion were inclined to oppose it because of anti-black stereotypes about Medicaid. "When we first started to collect postcards and signatures and support around this, I remember Latino organizers coming back to the office and [saying], 'We're not doing very well.' Because a lot of the folks [in] Latino communities were like, 'We don't want a handout. We work for what we earn. We're not asking for anything for free.'"

That's a late-stage benefit of a forty-year campaign to defund and degrade public benefits; in the end, they're so stigmatized that people whose lives would be transformed by them don't even want them for fear of sharing the stigma.

"I think politicians were pretty good at what they're always good at, right? Pitting communities against each other and using a lot of dog whistle politics around, like, 'Medicaid equates to black free-loading people,'" Ginny said with a sigh. "And unfortunately, that's resonating. Or hitting some of the underlying tension that already exists between African American and Latino communities."

The struggle for affordable health care for the working class continues in Texas and, as of summer 2020, twelve other states. Toward the end of our conversation, Ginny began to cry while recalling "a funeral of a woman who was the daughter of one of the first people I ever organized with. This African American man whose daughter died because she had lupus," a highly treatable disease.

"She had to wait and wait and wait until it got really, really bad. Then she could go to the emergency room. Then they would give her something, then they would turn her out. And she can never get ongoing care. She can never get medication or any treatment. She worked all sorts of low-wage jobs, from one to another. She has kids. And she's dead, at my age. In her late forties." Ginny's voice shook with both grief and rage. "People are dying because they would choose . . . a political victory over an actual victory that serves millions of people."

PAYING THE ULTIMATE PRICE

For Ron Pollack, a fifty-year leader in the fight for health care, housing, and other antipoverty measures, the person he won't forget is John, a Texan he met over twenty years ago, during the Clinton administration's lost battle for universal health care. "John told us the story about his wife," Ron told me. "He worked for a radio station. Wasn't making a lot of money. He talked about his wife being a very strong person. And she started getting stomach pains, and John would say to his wife, you know, 'We've got to see a doctor.'

"And she said, 'Well, we don't have the money to see a doctor. I'm gonna be okay.' And this persisted for months, until one day, she collapsed in excruciating pain, and she was taken by ambulance to a hospital. And they found this huge tumor in her stomach. And it was a very advanced tumor. And it was clear that she was going to pass away from this. And while she was at her deathbed, we were gonna start the bus trip across Texas to advocate for universal health care.

"And John was encouraged by his wife to get on the bus for three weeks to join us. And John said, 'Well, I don't feel comfortable leaving you like this.' She said, 'The last favor I have of you is that you join the bus trip. And tell my story, so that nobody experiences what we have experienced.'

"We were about halfway in the trip, and his wife died. And he flew back to bury her. And then he flew back to rejoin the bus. And he told his story at the White House. And of course, there wasn't a dry eye in the place," Ron said, his voice getting weak with the weight of the memory.

He cleared his throat. "So, yes, there have been quite a few people I have met—too numerous to count—who paid the ultimate price for their inability to get health coverage."

After a moment, I asked him about John's racial background.

"He was white."

Ron Pollack is not a household name by any means, but he has dedicated his life to extending the public web of protection around more Americans, and tens of millions of Americans are better off because he has. Ron founded the country's premier antihunger organization, the Food Research & Action Center, whose litigation and advocacy helped create the Special Supplemental Nutrition Assistance Program for Women, Infants and Children, including the food stamp program that feeds nearly forty million Americans. His organization Families USA was at the forefront of both the Clinton and Obama health care reform battles that eventually won health care for twenty-five million people, and at seventy-six years old, he has lately turned his passions to preventing evictions and ensuring affordable housing.

When I got the chance to talk with him, I wasn't so sure that he'd be willing to speak about the often-invisible headwinds of racism in his antipoverty efforts; I've known many a white liberal who was uncomfortable talking about racism's impact on politics. But he never shied away from naming racism, and when I asked him my final question, he shared with me the vision for America that has guided him through five decades of advocacy.

Ron said that, in his vision, "nobody in this country is deprived of the necessities of life—whether it's food, whether it's health care, whether it's housing—in a country that's as wealthy as ours."

To realize this vision, he said, "I wish there was a greater consciousness about how we're all in this together. For those people who are opposed to [government aid] out of an animus to people who look different than they are . . . that lack of social solidarity causes harm to their own communities.

"If we didn't have these sharp divisions based on race, we could make enormous progress in terms of making sure that people are not hurting as badly as they are, [or] deprived of what clearly are the necessities of life. And I would like to think it was possible if we had a sense of social solidarity."

Ron Pollack's diagnosis of the United States—that we suffer because our society was raised deficient in social solidarity—struck me as profoundly true, and, true to my optimistic nature, I suppose, I found the insight galvanizing. I began to think of all that a newfound solidarity could yield for our country, so young, so full of promise and power. Starting with health care and public college, I began to see the Solidarity Dividends waiting to be unlocked if more people would stop buying the old zero-sum story that elites use to keep us from taking care of one another. A Solidarity

Dividend is a public good—improved health care, affordable education, higher incomes—that can only be won when people come together across race to solve our common problems. My journey around the country has shown me that Solidarity Dividends are out there . . . if only we're willing to fight for them instead of fighting each other.

CHAPTER 4

IGNORING THE CANARY

WHEN JANICE AND ISAIAH TOMLIN MARRIED IN 1977, THEY promised each other that by their first anniversary, they'd become the first people in their families to own their own home. Janice's mother had always dreamed of owning a house, but segregation limited the options for black people in Wilmington, North Carolina. On the salaries of an elementary school teacher and an auto mechanic, the Tomlins saved up about $1,000 for a down payment and bought a bright blue two-bedroom house on Creecy Avenue for $11,500. They moved in right before their anniversary.

All the houses on Creecy have inviting front porches, and that's where Janice was sitting when I met her and Isaiah in the summer of 2020. A consumer attorney I've known for nearly two decades, Mike Calhoun, introduced me to them and connected us by a video call on their porch instead of the trip I'd planned to take to visit them, due to the pandemic. Janice told me about her introduction to the neighborhood: One night before they moved in, she was in the house painting over the dreadful lime green the previous owners had chosen for all the rooms, when she needed to make a call. The Tomlins' phone wasn't hooked up yet, but a nice white lady who lived next door offered to let her come in and use hers to call Isaiah. "And I thought, 'Gee, this is so nice. This is so kind,'" she recalled.

Her soon-to-be neighbor was out on the porch when Isaiah arrived later that night. Tall and deep mahogany–skinned, Isaiah was decidedly *not* what the white neighbor was expecting to see. Janice is fair-skinned and had just pressed her hair straight. "If you could have seen her face." Janice whistled as Isaiah laughed at the memory. "I will tell you that she was gone within months. Never spoke to us again, and was gone within months . . . and I thought, 'Oh, did we do that?'" She nodded to herself. "We did."

More black families moved in, and by the late 1990s, Janice said, it was a black neighborhood. Janice and Isaiah raised two children and kept improving their dream house. As the equity grew and the neighborhood changed, the phone calls started coming in from people marketing refinance loans. It just so happened that Janice was determined to send her children to Catholic school, and like many parents, she looked to their nest egg to help finance the tuition.

In the early spring of 1998, a company called Chase Mortgage Brokers had called the Tomlins multiple times, so Janice made an appointment to go in. "The very first meeting, the lady was so—I look back now—exceptionally kind. Just overbearing with kindness and patience," Janice recalled. "And I'm a question person. I ask a lot of questions. And she sat and she listened to me."

For all Janice's questions, however, there were some answers she wouldn't get from Chase—not until they showed up as evidence in a class-action predatory lending lawsuit. It turns out that Chase held itself out as a broker, someone a borrower hires to find them the best loan and who has a fiduciary duty (a legal obligation) to the borrower under North Carolina law. But Chase had a secret arrangement with just one lending company, Emergent. The exceptionally kind salesperson received kickbacks for every Emergent loan she sold, and no matter how low an interest rate a borrower might have qualified for, if the salesperson could sell them a higher-priced loan, she received even more of a kickback.

The salesperson at Chase also hid from Janice the extent of the fees that would be taken out of the Tomlins' home equity at signing. The included costs amounted to 12 percent of the loan on day one. Unbeknownst to them, the Tomlins had refinanced their dream home with a subprime mortgage with an annual interest rate in the double digits, unrelated to their credit scores.

This last point was important, because the official justification for the high cost of subprime mortgages was that higher costs were necessary for lenders to "price for the risk" of defaults by borrowers with poor credit. But lenders have no duty to sell you the best rate you qualify for—the limit is whatever they can get away with. I asked Janice, "Had you ever been late on your payments or missed a mortgage payment?"

Her warm voice turned firm. "Never."

"Never," I repeated. "That was very important to you?"

"Very important. Never late," she said, shaking her head emphatically.

Subprime would become a household word during the global financial crisis of 2008. I first came across the term when I started working at Demos in 2002 and when, as part of my outreach about our consumer debt research, I went to community meetings with dozens of borrowers just like the Tomlins, disproportionately black homeowners who were the first to be targeted by mortgage brokers and lenders. The loans are called *sub*prime because they're designed to be sold to borrowers who have lower-than-prime credit scores. That's the idea, but it wasn't the practice. An analysis conducted for the *Wall Street Journal* in 2007 showed that the majority of subprime loans were going to people *who could have qualified for less expensive prime loans.* So, if the loans weren't defined by the borrowers' credit scores, what did subprime loans all have in common? They had higher interest rates and fees, meaning they were more profitable for the lender, and because we're talking about five- and six-figure mortgage debt, those higher rates meant massively higher debt burdens for the borrower.

If you sell someone a prime-rate, 5 percent annual percentage rate (APR) thirty-year mortgage in the amount of $200,000, they'll pay you back an additional $186,512—93 percent of what they borrowed—for the privilege of spreading payments out over thirty years. If you can manage to sell that same person a subprime loan with a 9 percent interest rate, you can collect $379,328 on top of the $200,000 repayment, nearly twice what they borrowed. The public policy justification for allowing subprime loans was that they made the American Dream of homeownership possible for people who did not meet the credit standards to get a cheaper prime mortgage. But the subprime loans we started to see in the early 2000s were primarily marketed to existing homeowners, not people looking to buy—and they usually left the borrower worse off than before the loan. Instead of getting striving people into homeownership, the loans often wound up pushing existing homeowners out. The refinance loans stripped homeowners of equity they had built up over years of mortgage payments. That's why these diseased loans were tested first on the segment of Americans least respected by the financial sector and least protected by lawmakers: black and brown families.

At the closing, Janice saw that her interest rate was high, but the sales rep reassured her. "She told me . . . that I could come back in and we could lower the interest rate once I had paid on it for a certain amount of time. [I]t was like a perk for me; the interest rate will be lower. So, I thought, 'Well, this is good. It sounds like she's doing everything on my behalf.'"

Then there was the God part. Janice's sweet voice grew an edge as she said, "She had figured me out." Janice had told the broker that they were looking to refinance in order to free up money to pay for their children's Christian schooling. "And so, she talked about her Christian faith, which resonated with me. I remember the crosses that she had in the office."

The sales rep had touched Janice's hand and told her, "I know that God must have sent you to us. We're here for you."

Janice shook her head at the memory of "this person who is talking about God . . . and is trying to show me that she's giving me probably the best deal that I can get . . .

"I wasn't taught to doubt people who presented themselves as God-fearing people. So, I didn't doubt." She and Isaiah signed the paperwork.

Soon after, the address the Tomlins sent their monthly payments to began to change, frequently—the loans were being repeatedly sold—but, Janice says, "we were just trucking along and making the payments." It wasn't until Isaiah had a chance encounter with a local attorney that the Tomlins learned just how predatory their refinance loan was. That lawyer, Mallard "Mal" Maynard, was helping Isaiah recover a stolen tractor when Isaiah mentioned his refinance loan. (Unlike his wife, Isaiah had never had a good feeling about the salesperson or Chase.) Maynard asked if they still had the paperwork, and Janice did. "Of course I do," she'd told her husband. "I'm a schoolteacher. I keep papers."

Mal Maynard had joined our conversation on the porch. "I got copies of his paperwork and it just blew me away," he told me.

"What blew you away about it, Mal?" I asked. "It wasn't the monthly payment, right, because it sounds like the monthly payment was reasonable."

"It was the equity stripping. It was the yield-spread premiums. It was the origination fee. It was the duplicative fees. They had lots of duplicative fees with words that really made no sense as to what they were for." Chase had even charged the Tomlins a discount fee, which is what a borrower might pay a broker to get a lower rate than they qualify for—which was absurd, given that the Tomlins' rate was *higher* than they qualified for.

"But Mal, they weren't the only ones, right?"

"Oh, no. That was just the tip of the iceberg when I ran into Janice and Isaiah. Started looking at the Register of Deeds Office and tracking down dozens and then hundreds of other similar loans," Maynard said. He pointed to Janice. "She's being modest. She was the lead plaintiff [for] thirteen hundred folks [whose homes] she helped save . . . who had gone through this same thing."

Overcoming their shame at being named plaintiffs in a class-action lawsuit wasn't easy for Janice and Isaiah. "In the courtroom . . . there would be someone to make a mockery of my ignorance. That was really hard to swallow," Janice admitted. "But I knew that, in the end, there would be others who would benefit from it."

With the relative rarity of a lightning strike—an available and dogged lawyer, a well-timed suit in a state with good consumer protections, and a particularly corrupt and inept defendant—the Tomlins saved their home and protected more than a thousand other working- and middle-class homeowners in their state. Had more black families targeted by subprime lenders in those early years found the Tomlins' happy ending, history would have turned. The mortgage market would have learned its lesson about subprime mortgages earlier in the 2000s, and the worst excesses would have been checked before they spun out of control and toppled the entire economy, causing $19.2 trillion in lost household wealth and eight million lost jobs—and that was just in the United States. The earliest predatory mortgage lending victims, disproportionately black, were the canaries in the coal mine, but their warning went unheeded.

The blast radius of foreclosures from the 2008 explosion on Wall Street (and the ensuing Great Recession) was far-reaching and permanent. By way of comparison, in 2001, about 183,000 home foreclosures were reported across the nation. By 2008, a record 983,000. In 2010, a new record: more than 1,178,000. An accounting on the tenth anniversary of the crash showed 5.6 million foreclosed homes during the Great Recession. Although homeowners of color were represented out of proportion to their numbers in society, the majority of these foreclosed homes belonged to white people.

DO NOT SAY "I LOST MY HOME"

Amy Rogers is a white woman whose life has been forever changed because of the Great Recession. In 2001, she and her husband bought their first home, a three-bedroom house she describes as funky and long on character. She had her own savings and the money her parents had left her ($50,000) to put into the purchase to keep their mortgage payments modest. By 2005, Amy had a great job for the first time in her life, one with a good salary and benefits, working for her county government. Then she discovered that without her knowledge, her husband had pulled all the equity out of the house and used it for his own purposes. Shocked, she began divorce proceedings. In 2007, the divorce became final, and Amy got the house refinanced in her own name. But she had to buy out her husband's debt to do so. "Having had the house for seven years," she said, "we owed more than we had paid. I took on $275,000 or so of debt."

As it turns out, the booming county Amy worked for was the home of the city whose fortunes had risen with the rise of the financial sector in the 1990s and 2000s, nicknamed Banktown. Charlotte, North Carolina, was the headquarters for large national banks that were growing by leaps and bounds in the lead-up to the crisis, including Bank of America and Wachovia. But the year after her divorce became final, all the construction of houses and office towers ground to a halt. The city began to cut back. By 2009, government employees like Amy were feeling it hard. "The first thing they did was reduce our benefits, and take away our holidays, and put us on furlough without pay. Then they gave us pay cuts. Then, after amputating us one limb at a time, I got fired."

She was able to get a federal program called COBRA to extend her health insurance, but the monthly cost soared from a subsidized $80 to $779. Her mortgage payment, on a conventional thirty-year mortgage, stayed at $1,200 a month—manageable, but just barely, based on unemployment insurance, alimony, and the little bits of income she could pull together through freelance jobs.

As part of its belt-tightening, the local government reassessed properties and revalued Amy's $255,000 house at $414,000, which almost tripled her property taxes. Six months after she was laid off, Amy realized she wasn't going to be able to manage both her mortgage and her increased property taxes. Things were "starting to snowball," she said.

She called the owner of her mortgage, Wells Fargo, and told them that although she had not yet been late with a payment, her financial situation had changed and she wanted to sign up for one of the programs it offered to reduce borrowers' mortgage payments. "Then they start putting me through the wringer," Amy said.

Although she had no credit problems, Wells Fargo told her she needed to attend credit counseling. "Okay, fine, I go," Amy said. "I went to the 'Save Your Housing' fair. I went to the Housing Finance Agency. I went and did every single thing that was out there to do. Wells Fargo had me jumping through hoops for three years." The Obama administration had started a number of programs, she recalled, to enable people to extend the term of their mortgage or, in some cases, reduce the interest rate or even the principal. "I went for everything," Amy said. "And everywhere I went, they blocked me and said, 'You can't apply for this [program] if you're under consideration for that. You can't apply for that while you're under consideration for this. Oh, that program is over.' And it went around and around for months and months and months.

"The minute you go and you ask for help, even if you're not late [making your payments], your credit score drops one hundred points. So, what that meant was that my Exxon card that I'd had since 1984, [which] had six or seven hundred dollars on it for oil changes and tires—all of a sudden, they jack up the interest rate to thirty-five percent. I've never been late, but I'm now a 'high-risk borrower.'

"My unemployment's running out, and I'm selling jewelry to make the mortgage payments. And I realize they're going to take the house anyway." Amy put her home up for sale. "I owed altogether two hundred seventy-five thousand, and we brought them offers within ten thousand of that, and Wells Fargo turned every one of them down." The bank would not accept a sale price any less than the full amount owed, nor would they take possession of the house instead of foreclosing on it.

"I did everything I could to avoid foreclosure," said Amy, "knowing what that would do to my credit and my employability. So, [at this point,] I'm fifty-five years old. I'm doing piecemeal work everywhere and paying self-employment tax and COBRA and just going down in flames."

In 2013, Wells Fargo finally foreclosed on Amy Rogers. She was one of 679,923 Americans to experience foreclosure that year. But the shocks didn't end there. When her house went up for auction, Wells Fargo bought it—from itself—for $304,000. Why such a high price for a house that was selling for $275,000? "Because every time they sent me a letter from a lawyer or made a phone call, they billed me," Amy said. "They wanted to recoup all their costs to foreclose on me."

As the final step in the foreclosure process, "the sheriff in his big hat and his big car drives up to your house in broad damn daylight, comes and knocks on your door, and serves you with an eviction notice," said Amy. "That is a dark day."

She sold or gave away most of her belongings and moved into a small rental condo, where she lived until she had to move again in 2017. When Amy shared these details a year later, she said the rent on her new place was affordable, but the run-down neighborhood was gentrifying, so she feared the landlord would soon raise the rent. "I pay over ten thousand dollars a year in rent," she said. "I earn about twenty-four thousand.

"When they foreclosed on me for the house," said Amy, "they got [everything]. I got zero. They ruined my credit. And they ruined my employability, because any employer you go to work for now does a credit check on you. I couldn't get a job for ten dollars an hour in Costco. I tried.

"I paid into that house for thirteen years. I've worked every day of my life since I'm seventeen years old. And now, today, I'm sixty-three years old, I'm unemployable, I work three part-time jobs, and I'm praying I can last long enough to get Medicare so I'll have some health coverage."

Every part of Amy's story was one that I knew well from my re-search and advocacy at Demos, from the jacked-up credit card rate, to the insufficient foreclosure prevention programs (I lobbied staff at the US Treasury Department to improve them), to the job dis-crimination against people with weak credit (we wrote a bill ban-ning the practice). Not a single part of her story surprised me, but it moved me still. I was grateful that she'd been willing to share her story with me, knowing it would be made public. There's so much shame involved in being in debt. In my experience with the bankers on the other end, however, shame is hard to find, even over their discriminatory and deceptive practices. Amy sighed. "I've kept it under wraps for ten years," she said, "too afraid of the way the world would perceive me.

"If I could leave anybody who's gone through this with one

message," she said, "it is this: Do not say, 'I lost my house.' You did not lose your house. It was taken away from you."

The people who took Amy's house could do so with impunity in 2013 only because they had been doing it to homeowners of color for over a decade already, and had built the practices, corporate cultures, and legal and regulatory loopholes to enable that plunder back when few people cared. Subprime mortgages and the attitude of lender irresponsibility they fomented would, we now know, later spread throughout the housing market. But to truly understand where the crisis began, we have to go back earlier than the 1990s, to the 1930s, and the reason it was so easy for lenders to target homeowners of color in the first place.

A BRIEF HISTORY OF RACIAL EXCLUSION FROM HOMEOWNERSHIP

"We think of the New Deal [in the 1930s] and all the great things that came out of it—and there were many—but what we don't talk about nearly as often is the extent to which those great things were structured in ways that made sure people of color didn't have access to them," said Debby Goldberg, a vice president of the National Fair Housing Alliance. I worked closely with the advocates at NFHA back in the early 2000s. Debby is an advocate who spends her days defending Americans' right to fair housing, and she has an encyclopedic knowledge of the history of US homeownership, and the housing policies that had paved the way for the subprime mortgage crisis.

In 1933, during the Great Depression, the US government created the Home Owners' Loan Corporation, which drew maps of the largest cities in the country and used different colors to show the level of supposed investment risk in individual neighborhoods. A primary basis for defining a neighborhood's risk was the race of its residents, with people of color considered the riskiest—even though there was no proof that this would be the case. Neighborhoods of color were identified by red shading to warn lenders not to invest there—the birth of redlining. (A typical assessment reads: "The neighborhood is graded 'D' because of its concentration of negroes, but the section may improve to a third class area as this element is forced out.")

The redlining maps were subsequently used by the Federal Housing Administration, created in 1934. In its early years, Goldberg explained, the FHA subsidized the purchase of housing "in a way that made it very easy for working-class white people, who had previously been renters and may never have had any expectation of becoming a homeowner, to move to the suburbs and become a homeowner because it was often cheaper than renting. Both the structure and the interest rate of the mortgage made it possible for people to do that with very little savings and relatively low income.

"But the FHA would not make or guarantee mortgages for borrowers of color," she said. "It would guarantee mortgages for developers who were building subdivisions, but only on the condition that they include deed restrictions preventing any of those homes from being sold to people of color. Here we have this structure that facilitated . . . white homeownership, and therefore the creation of white wealth at a heretofore unprecedented scale—and [that] explicitly prevented people of color from having those same benefits. To a very large degree, this was the genesis of the incredible racial wealth gap we have today." In 2019, the most recent available authoritative data, the typical white family in America had about $184,000 in wealth, mostly from homeownership—that's eight times that of black families ($23,000) and almost five times that of Latinx families ($38,000). That kind of wealth is self-perpetuating, because wealth is where history shows up in your wallet. I thought of Amy Rogers, who on a modest income had still been able to afford a house with a low monthly payment largely because of $50,000 from her parents. Because of the racist exclusion from US wealth-building policies, white high school dropouts typically have more family wealth than do black college graduates!

Learning this history was crucial to me in my early days at Demos. In order to help craft new laws to change the world we inhabited, I needed to understand how government decisions had shaped it. I underwent a steady process of unlearning some of the myths about progressive victories like the New Deal and the GI Bill, achievements that I understood to have built the great American middle class. The government agencies most responsible for the vast increase in home ownership—from about 40 percent of Americans in 1920 to about 62 percent in 1960—were also responsible for the exclusion of people of color from this life-changing economic opportunity. Of all the African Americans in the United States during the decades between 1930 and 1960, fewer than 2 percent were able to get a home loan from the government.

The civil rights movement brought changes to housing laws, but lending practices changed more slowly. For instance, although the Fair Housing Act of 1968 outlawed racially discriminatory practices by banks, it would take another twenty-four years for the Federal Reserve System, the central bank of the United States, to monitor and (spottily) enforce the law. And in the meantime, racial discrimination in lending has persisted.

THE BANKS' INCENTIVES TO CHEAT

In the aftermath of the financial crash of 2008, Doris Dancy became a witness in a federal fair lending lawsuit based on what she saw as a credit manager for Wells Fargo in Memphis during the housing boom. "My job was to find as many potential borrowers for Wells Fargo as possible. We were put under a lot of pressure to call these individuals repeatedly and encourage them to come into the office to apply for a loan. Most—eighty percent or more—of the leads on the lists I was given were African American." The leads came from lists of Wells Fargo customers who had credit cards, car loans, or home equity loans with the company.

"We were supposed to try and refinance these individuals into new, expensive subprime loans with high interest rates and lots of fees and costs," Dancy explained. "The way we were told to sell these loans was to explain that we were eliminating the customer's old debts by consolidating their existing debts into one new one. This was not really true—we were not getting rid of the customer's existing debts; we were actually just giving them a new, more expensive loan that put their house at risk.

"Our district manager pressured the credit managers in my office to convince our leads to apply for a loan, even if we knew they could not afford the loan or did not qualify for the loan. . . . I know that Wells Fargo violated its own underwriting guidelines in order to make loans to these customers.

"Many of the mostly African American customers who came into the offices were not experienced in applying for loans. . . . Our district manager told us to conceal the details of the loan. He thought that these customers could be 'talked into anything.' The way he pressured us to do all of these unethical things was as aggressive as a wolf. There was no compassion for these individuals who came to us trusting our advice."

Mario Taylor, another Wells Fargo credit manager in Memphis, explained how the bank applied pressure to its almost entirely African American prospects. "We were instructed to make as many as thirty-five calls an hour and to call the same borrower multiple times each day," he said. "Some branch managers told us how to mislead borrowers. For example, we were told to make 'teaser rate' loans without informing the borrower that the loan was adjustable. . . . Some managers . . . changed pay stubs and used Wite-Out on documents to alter the borrower's income so it would look like the customer qualified for the loan. Borrowers were not told about prepayment penalties [or] . . . about astronomical fees that were added to the loan and that Wells Fargo profited from."

A common misperception then and now is that subprime loans were being sought out by financially irresponsible borrowers with bad credit, so the lenders were simply appropriately pricing the loans higher to offset the risk of default. And in fact, subprime loans were more likely to end up in default. If a black homeowner finally answered Mario Taylor's dozenth call and ended it possessing a mortgage that would turn out to be twice as expensive as the prime one he started with, is it any wonder that it would quickly become unaffordable? This is where the age-old stereotypes equating black people with risk—an association explicitly drawn in red ink around America's black neighborhoods for most of the twentieth century—obscured the plain and simple truth: what was risky wasn't the borrower; it was the *loan*.

Camille Thomas, a loan processor, testified that "many of these customers could have qualified for less expensive or prime loans, but because Wells Fargo Financial only made subprime loans, managers had a financial incentive to put borrowers into subprime loans with high interest rates and fees even when they qualified for better-priced loans." In some markets, black borrowers were eight times more likely to get a subprime loan than white borrowers with similar financial histories. And more than half of the $2.5 trillion in subprime loans made between 2000 and 2007 also went to buyers who qualified for safer, cheaper prime loans.

The bank's incentives to cheat its customers were rich. Elizabeth Jacobson, a loan officer from 1998 to 2007, explained the incentive system. "My pay was based on commissions and fees I got from making [subprime] loans. . . . In 2004, I grossed more than seven hundred thousand in sales commissions," nearly one million in 2020 dollars. "The commission and referral system at Wells Fargo was set up in a way that made it more profitable for a loan officer to refer a prime customer for a subprime loan than make the prime loan directly to the customer." Underwriters also made more money from a subprime than a prime loan.

Looking at these numbers, one could be tempted to minimize the role of racism and chalk it up to greed instead. I'm sure that most of the people involved in the industry would claim not to have a racist bone in their body—in fact, I heard those exact words from representatives of lending companies in the aftermath of the crash. But history might counter: What is racism without greed? It operates on multiple levels. Individual racism, whether conscious or unconscious, gives greedy people the moral permission to exploit others in ways they never would with people with whom they empathized. Institutional racism of the kind that kept the management ranks of lenders and regulators mostly white furthered this social distance. And then structural racism both made it easy to prey on people of color due to segregation and eliminated the accountability when disparate impacts went unheeded. Lenders, brokers, and investors targeted people of color because they thought they could get away with it. Because of racism, they could.

So much profit and so little accountability. AmeriQuest, BancorpSouth, Citigroup, Washington Mutual, and many other banks and financial companies contributed to a wave of foreclosures that shrank the wealth of the average African American family by more than half between 2005 and 2009 and of the average Latinx family by more than two-thirds.

WE COULD HAVE STOPPED IT

There was a time—years, in fact—when the epidemic of home foreclosures could have been stopped. Bank regulators and federal policy-makers were well aware of what was happening in communities of color, but despite pleas from local officials and community groups, they did nothing to stop the new lenders and their new tactics that left so many families without a home. Between 1992 and 2008, state officials took more than nine thousand legal, regulatory, and policy actions to try to stop the predatory mortgage lenders that were devastating their communities and their tax bases. But Washington wouldn't listen. The Federal Reserve—"the one entity with the authority to regulate risky lending practices by all mortgage lenders"—took no action at all, and the Office of the Comptroller of the Currency, the regulator in charge of national bank practices, took one action: preemption, to make sure that no state's consumer protections applied to its national banks.

In the virtually all-white realm of federal bank regulators and legislators, there was a blindness in those early years. Lisa Donner is a slight woman whose speech is peppered with almost involuntary little laughs, which I decided, after years of working in the consumer protection trenches with her, was a defense mechanism, a release valve for the pressure of having seen all the injustice she's seen. She got her start organizing working-class New Yorkers of color around affordable housing and foreclosure prevention with the Association of Community Organizations for Reform Now (ACORN) thirty years ago. She's now the executive director of Americans for Financial Reform, the David founded in the wake of the crash to take on Wall Street's lobbying Goliath and create a new regulatory structure to prevent a crash from happening again. Lisa has sat across the table from more financial regulators and bankers than probably anyone else in the country. I got in touch with her to reminisce about what it was like in the early days of the subprime phenomenon, when families like the Tomlins were being targeted, block by block.

The regulators were "just refusing to see that there was a problem at all," Lisa said with one of her little laughs. "Because it wasn't their neighbors or their neighborhood or people who looked like them, or people they knew, in the elite decision-making circles."

I have many such memories, but I'll never forget a meeting with a young blond Senate banking committee staffer in 2003. After hearing our research presentation, she said with a sad little shake of her head, "the problem was we put these people into houses when we shouldn't have."

I marveled at the inversion of agency in her phrasing. Who was the "we"? Not the hardworking strivers who had finally gotten their fingers around the American Dream despite every barrier and obstacle. No, the "we" was well-intentioned people in government—undoubtedly white, in her mental map. Never mind that most of the predatory loans we were talking about weren't intended to help people purchase homes, but rather, were draining equity from existing homeowners. From 1998 to 2006, the majority of subprime mortgages created were for refinancing, and less than 10 percent were for first-time home buyers. It was still a typical refrain, redolent of long-standing stereotypes about people of color being unable to handle money—a tidy justification for denying them ways to obtain it.

Lisa Donner understood the work that race was doing in shifting blame for irresponsible lending and deception onto the borrower. "Race was a part of weaponizing the 'It's the borrower's fault' language," she said to me.

Such financial malfeasance was allowed to flourish because the people who were its first victims didn't matter nearly as much as the profits their pain generated. But the systems set up to exploit one part of our society rarely stay contained. Once the financial industry and regulators were able to let racist stereotypes and indifference justify massive profits from unfair and risky practices, the brakes were off for good. The rest of the mortgage market, with its far more numerous white borrowers, was there for the taking. Subprime went mainstream.

In late 2007, when interest rates rose and housing prices started falling, the mortgage market at the center of the economy began to crumble. By the time the housing market reached bottom, housing prices would fall by over 30 percent and all five of the major investment houses would either go bankrupt or be absorbed in a fire sale.

With the banks and the houses went the jobs. In the recession that followed, "people were losing their jobs or having their hours cut back," Debby Goldberg recalled. "In that situation, you had mortgages that were perfectly safe and [that,] in ordinary circumstances, should have been sustainable, but people just couldn't afford them anymore because they had lost income. And they couldn't sell their home because home values were going down all across the country." It was a vicious circle. This third wave of the financial disaster crested in 2008–2009, the period generally designated as the Great Recession, but the devastation that wave created continues even now.

Millions of American families and communities have been permanently scarred because of the financial industry's actions in the 2000s. While the country's GDP and employment numbers rebounded before the pandemic struck another blow, the damage at the household level has been permanent. Of families who lost their houses through dire events such as job loss or foreclosure, over two-thirds will probably never own a home again. Because of our globally interconnected economy, the Great Recession altered lives in every country in the world.

And all of it was preventable, if only we had paid attention earlier to the financial fires burning through black and brown communities across the nation. Instead, the predatory practices were allowed to continue until the disaster had engulfed white communities, too—and only then, far too late, was it recognized as an emergency. There is no question that the financial crisis hurt people of color first and worst. And yet the majority of the people it damaged were white. This is the dynamic we've seen over and over again throughout our country's history, from the drained public pools, to the shuttered public schools, to the overgrown yards of vacant homes.

DROP A LITTLE GOOD IN THE HOLE

I'll never forget a trip I took to the Mount Pleasant neighborhood in Cleveland, Ohio. On a leafy street, residents told me how, a few years back, house by house, each homeowner—over 90 percent of them black, with a few Latinx and South Asian immigrants—had opened an envelope, answered a knock on the door, or taken a call from someone with an offer to help consolidate their debt or lower their bills. In the ensuing years, with quiet shame and in loud public hearings—with supportive aldermen, pastors, and lawyers outmatched by the indifference of bankers and regulators with the power to help them—residents had fought to keep their homes. But by 2007, the block I was on had only two or three houses still in the hands of their rightful owners. I excused myself from the group and walked around the corner, barely getting out of their sight in time to fall to my knees, crying, chest heaving. It was the weight of the history, the scale of the theft, and how powerless we had proven to change any of it. These were properties that meant everything to people whose ancestors—grandparents, in some cases—had been sold as property. To this day, it's hard for me to think about it without emotion.

That's why, as I looked at the Tomlins smiling at each other on their porch more than a decade later, it was like I'd slipped into the world as it could have been—as it *should* have been. I felt like I was glimpsing not only an alternate past in which more borrowers had their just resolution, but maybe an alternate society in which more people had their values.

I was asking Janice and Isaiah about their court case when the lawyer Mal Maynard jumped in. "I gotta throw in my two cents here. Of course, Janice is one of my all-time heroes. One of the greatest days I've ever had in court was in Winston Salem in . . . the North Carolina Business Court, which is always a bad [place] for consumer cases. There was a judge who was really famous for being very, very hard on the class actions, especially when they were filed by consumers." After Janice took the stand, the skeptical judge asked her, basically, why she was there—why she was willing to swear an oath to represent the interests of over a thousand people she didn't know.

Janice continued in her own words: "I just remember telling [the judge] that every morning when I walked into my classroom before we started our day, I taught my second graders to place their hands on their hearts and quietly say the Pledge of Allegiance.

"And I had taught them that when you give allegiance to something, you say that 'I honor this' and that 'I have faith in it.' And I knew that if I taught that to my children, that I best be living by it myself."

Mal continued: "And from that moment forward, she transformed Judge Tennille. She really did. He believed in us, and he believed in our case from that point forward. There was still a lot of hard-fought litigation, but he knew, and Janice convinced him, that this was really legitimate, heartfelt work that was being done by her and by the lawyers in the case."

A far-off look in Janice's eyes made me wonder what else had been guiding her that day. Finally she said, "My daddy used to say, 'Drop a little good in the hole before you go.' That sticks with me. I was just trying to be a good citizen. And I was just letting that judge know that I had no other reason to come here but that . . . Because somebody's name had to be there. Did I want it to be our names? No, I did not."

The Tomlins' courageous act of solidarity with other ripped-off homeowners paid dividends. Their lawsuit for deceptive, unfair, and excessive fees and breach of fiduciary duty to the borrower succeeded in 2000, with a settlement of about $10 million. "So, borrowers all over North Carolina got checks, thanks to Janice and Isaiah," Mal said with pride.

Janice allowed a small smile. "That's a lot of people being served. You know? It was more than worth our names being in the newspaper. We should have been so very embarrassed at the end of that, but I wasn't, because I felt like I had put a little good in the hole."

CHAPTER 5

NO ONE FIGHTS ALONE

O N AUGUST 4, 2017, A GROUP OF WORKERS AT A NISSAN auto factory in Canton, Mississippi, held a historic vote about whether they should join the United Auto Workers (UAW) Union, a move that would bring their wages, job security, and benefits closer to those of the unionized factories in the Midwest. Prounion activists had spent ten years organizing and campaigning, but in the end, their side failed by a margin of five hundred votes.

When I first read about this—autoworkers voting against unionizing—it struck me as a "man bites dog" story. I grew up in the Midwest, where driving a foreign car was seen as low treason, where the people who built American cars had the best jobs around, and where everybody knew that this was because the Big Three (GM, Chrysler, and Ford) had to negotiate with workers through the United Auto Workers. News coverage about the Nissan "no" vote referenced racial divisions in the plant, and I felt I had to learn more about what had happened. I flew into Medgar

Evers Airport in Jackson, Mississippi, and drove up I-55 until I saw the bright white Nissan water tower come up on the horizon. The plant itself soon came into view. Not many windows, set back from the highway, it extended for four miles of road.

After circling the plant, I continued driving a few miles more to the worker center, where I was to meet Sanchioni Butler, the UAW organizer. The worker center was in a storefront in a strip mall that held vacant stores and a health clinic. When I walked in, I told a man sitting at the front desk that I had an appointment with Sanchioni, and he asked me to have a seat. In the lobby were a coffee machine, a small fridge, and a dozen chairs around the walls, half full with workers from the plant: four black men, two black women, and one white man, standard-issue Styrofoam coffee cups in most hands. They were all postshift, leaning back heavily in their folding chairs—though, as we talked, their voices regained the energy their bodies had given up for the day. Most were wearing black T-shirts with REMEMBER on the front and a list on the back: INJURED COWORKERS, FROZEN PENSIONS, INEQUALITY FOR PATHWAYS WORKERS, REDUCED HEALTH CARE, WORKERS FIRED WITHOUT CAUSE, along with a name, DERRICK WHITING—a man who had collapsed on the plant floor and later died. Some wore a similar shirt with a positive message: WE DESERVE: A NEGOTI-ATED PENSION, FAIRNESS FOR PATHWAYS, A SAFER PLANT, BETTER HEALTH CARE PLANS, UNION REPRESENTATION. One woman's shirt had a pair of clasped hands and the words NO ONE FIGHTS ALONE emblazoned across the back.

I introduced myself. Melvin, a black man with a quick smile, an obvious charmer, rose to shake my hand first and adjusted the chairs so that I could sit in the middle of everyone. Earl was the oldest of the bunch, with gray in his mustache and a sharp crease in his pants that set his attire apart from the work pants and jeans around the room. Rhonda was the youngest-looking person in the room, wearing a gray-and-black camouflage hat with an American flag on it. The daughter of a union worker, she had kind eyes and a dimple that appeared with her tight-lipped smile. Johnny was a tall white man in a cutoff shirt with a sleeve of tattoos and a contrary attitude. (When I asked him what he did at the plant, he said wryly, "It's the same job. I've been doing the same job for fourteen years.")

Over the course of the first morning I spent in the worker center, half a dozen more people would come through and join the conversation. Almost all were black men and women; there were a few white guys, and, I noticed, no white women. The name Chip came up a couple of times, and I jotted it down: a white guy who had caved to pressure in the final weeks and, they said, switched sides. Talking to the group about what problems they hoped a union would solve, I heard about their having to pay thousands of dollars in deductibles before their health coverage kicked in. I heard about the frozen pensions for those who had been with Nissan in the beginning, when benefits were more generous, and the insecure 401(k) for everybody else. I heard stories of women eight months pregnant being denied light duty and forced to lift fifty-pound parts. I heard, in a level of detail I wish I could forget, about the way an assembly line part can tear off a finger, yanking it away and taking the tendon with it, up and out, all the way up to the elbow.

It was jarring to hear auto plant jobs described this way, as everybody knows that manufacturing jobs are the iconic "good jobs" of the American middle class. But the truth is factory jobs used to be terrible jobs, with low pay and dangerous conditions, until the people who needed those jobs to survive banded together, often overcoming violent oppression, to demand wholesale change to entire industries: textiles, meatpacking, steel, automobiles. The early-twentieth-century fights to make good jobs out of dangerous ones—the fights, in fact, to create the American middle class—could never have been waged alone. Desperate for work and easily exploited, workers had power only in numbers. One worker could ask for a raise and be shown the door, behind which dozens of people were lined up to take his place. But what remade American work in the industrial era was the fact that companies didn't face individual pleas for improvement; they faced mass work stoppages, slowdowns, armed protests, and strikes that forced employers to the bargaining table. The result was jobs with better pay, benefits, and safety practices and upward mobility for generations of Americans to come. These victories were possible only when people recognized their common struggles and linked arms.

And linking arms for those workers usually meant forming a union. The first time I heard the word *union,* it was from my father's best friend, Jim Dyson, a man I called Uncle Jimmy. Uncle Jimmy was a union man in my neighborhood on the South Side of Chicago, and he wore the power of that backing like a wool coat in winter. He exuded pride in his work. His family had things that I knew, even as a child, were prized—vacations to the dunes in Wisconsin every year, braces for his daughter when the dentist said she needed them, a good-sized house that we all gathered in to watch football on Sundays. I remember once being in the backseat of my dad's car and watching Uncle Jimmy through the open window, in a neighborhood not our own. He was standing on the street, joking and backslapping with a group of Polish- and Italian-accented men. I'd never seen that before. Later, I would put it together: Uncle Jimmy was in a union, the only place where men like that would know and trust one another in segregated Chicago.

THE COLOR LINE ON THE JOB

At the Canton worker center, the men and women had that same ease as they told me a shared story of the way the company kept workers apart and vying for positions at the plant. They spoke of a very clear, though informal, ranking of jobs at Nissan. First, there was a hierarchy of job status. On the top tier were the so-called Legacy workers, who started at Nissan when the company first came to Canton, making front-page news by offering a pay and benefits package that was generous by Mississippi standards. A few years later, the company contracted out those exact same jobs to subcontractors like Kelly Services, at about half the pay, a practice I still can't believe is legal. Kelly is a temporary employment agency, and Nissan classifies the jobs as such—but I spoke to workers who had been full-time "temps" for more than five years. These workers, earning about $12 an hour with no benefits, were on the bottom tier. In between the top and bottom tiers were workers on a program Nissan called Pathway, where temp workers were put on a path to full-time status, though never at the Legacy level of pay and benefits. The result was that thousands of workers did the same job with the same skill, side by side on the line, but management kept the power to assign workers to different categories—meaning different pay, different benefits, different work rules.

Labor experts call this kind of division a tactic: create a sense of hierarchy and you motivate workers to compete with one another to please the bosses and get to the next category up, instead of fighting together to get rid of the categories and create a common, improved work environment for everyone. Though the company has been reluctant to publicly release exact numbers about its staffing, estimates put the number of nonemployee Pathway and temporary workers at the plant as high as 40 percent. The nonemployee workers were not allowed to cast a ballot in the union drive, which silenced the voice of the lowest-paid and most precarious workers. As Sanchioni Butler would later tell me, "I think that it's fair to say that if I'm working side by side with you, we're doing the same work. I think I should be paid the same for sure. . . . That's the cry of the two-tier Pathway person."

The workers also spoke of an invisible ladder of difficulty that stretched from the assembly line, where workers maneuvered parts at the relentless pace of machines, to the "offline" jobs—for instance, as predelivery inspectors (PDI) who walk around a finished car checking off items on a list. Earl wanted me to understand the difference between being on the line and being offline: "Those PDI jobs are so cush, those folks can leave work and go straight to the happy hour—they don't even have to go home and shower. That's how you can tell how cush the job is." Everyone I spoke to—white, black, management, and production—admitted that the positions got whiter as the jobs got easier and better paid.

In the face of a possible cross-racial organizing drive, it seemed to be a company strategy to make white workers feel different from, better than, the black majority in the plant. Rhonda had been working in the physically demanding "trim" section for years. When I asked her about conversations with white workers in her section, she shrugged. "I don't have any white workers in my section."

After hearing the descriptions of the racial ranking when it came to the most physically taxing jobs, I had a hard time squaring that reality with one of the other things I heard repeated in my conversations with workers, particularly the antiunion white workers: that management said the black workers were lazy, and that was why they wanted a union. If they were so lazy, why were they doing all the hardest, most relentless and dangerous jobs, the ones that also happened to be the lowest-paying?

When I finally got in to see her, I asked Sanchioni Butler, the UAW organizer, about this contradiction. A black woman with a determined expression, Sanchioni was once a "regular hourly worker" in parts distribution at a unionized Ford plant in Memphis,

Tennessee, but she signed up one day for a UAW class on organizing and got hooked. "I'm second-generation union," she told me with some pride. Knowing the difference that her father's good union job had made in her family, she moved deeper south to help factory workers organize in Georgia and then Canton, where she'd been for the whole Nissan campaign. She said the claim that the black workers were lazy was something she came up against all the time, and to deal with it, she would ask the person to compare that stereotype with what they saw at the plant: "I'll say, 'Okay, let's be real. You're working on the assembly line. You have to keep up with the line; it's constant, repetitive movement. How can you be lazy in a job like that?' And then they'll say, 'You know what, you're right.' But [I have to get] them to think about the seed that the company is dropping to divide these people."

THE ZERO SUM AT WORK

In the two-hundred-year history of American industrial work, there's been no greater tool against collective bargaining than employers' ability to divide workers by gender, race, or origin, stoking suspicion and competition across groups. It's simple: if your boss can hire someone else cheaper, or threaten to, you have less leverage for bargaining. In the nineteenth century, employers' ability to pay black workers a fraction of white wages made whites see free black people as threats to their livelihood. In the early twentieth century, new immigrants were added to this competitive dynamic, and the result was a zero sum: the boss made more profit; one group had new, worse work, and the other had none. In the war years, men would protest the employment of women. Competition across demographic groups was the defining characteristic of the American labor market, but the stratification only helped the employer. The solution for workers was to bargain collectively: to band together across divisions and demand improvements that lifted the floor for everyone.

Only when external pressures forced racial and gender integration on unions—labor shortages during World War II and the Great Migration of African Americans into the industrial Midwest put more women and people of color in factories—did the barriers begin to fall. Unions finally began integrating. And it was in these years of cross-racial organizing that unions experienced a Solidarity Dividend, with membership climbing to levels that let unions set wages across large sectors of the economy. More and more of the country's workforce joined a union on the job, with membership reaching a high-water mark of one out of every three workers in the 1950s. The victories these unions won reshaped work for us all. The forty-hour workweek, overtime pay, employer health insurance and retirement benefits, worker compensation—all these components of a "good job" came from collective bargaining and union advocacy with governments in the late 1930s and '40s. And the power to win these benefits came from solidarity—black, white, and brown, men and women, immigrant and native-born.

THE DECLINE OF LABOR

Of course, that was then. It's hard to find a good union job today, and it's not because nonunion labor is so rich with benefits. Almost half of adult workers are classified as "low-wage," earning about $10 an hour, or $18,000 a year, on average. A person with the same experience and education earns 11 percent more for the same job if they're in a union. After the 1950s peak, the share of workers covered by a collectively bargained work contract has fallen every decade. Today, it's just one out of every sixteen private-sector workers. I was born at a time when the loss of union factory jobs on the South Side of Chicago was changing everything: families split up and moved, stores closed and schools cut programs, folks turned to illegal work, and neighbors stopped sitting on their porches after the streetlights came on. As factory unions weakened, it felt like everything else did, too.

So, as I sat and listened to the men and women at the Nissan worker center describe the future they had glimpsed, fought for, and lost, I knew that what they'd been struggling for could have made a difference in their lives and in the trajectory of inequality in America. The share of workers in a union has directly tracked the share of the country's income that goes to the middle class, and as union density has declined, the portion going to the richest Americans has increased in step.

And so, the questions loom: If joining a union is such a demonstrable good, why are unions on the decline? Why would any worker hoping to better her lot in life oppose a union in a vote?

Labor's breaking point came over the course of the late 1970s when businesses had begun to freely flout the laws protecting workers' rights to organize, accepting fines and fees as a tolerable cost of doing business. Today, one in five unionizing drives results in charges that employers illegally fired workers for union activity, despite federal protections. It's illegal to threaten to close the workplace rather than be forced to bargain with your employees, but the majority of businesses facing union drives do it anyway. The Nissan employees attested that they heard those threats on constant repeat from the plant's TV screens and loudspeakers, and the National Labor Relations Board (NLRB) issued a complaint against Nissan about illegal tactics.

A backdrop of economic insecurity makes these tactics more powerful. A job—no matter what the pay or conditions—can seem better than the ever-present threat of no job at all. And it's true that labor's enemies were aided and abetted by new rules of global competition and technological change that made American jobs less secure. As large American companies began to automate and look to nations in the Global South for labor in the 1970s and '80s, the threat and reality of job losses proved powerful in forcing unions to make concessions and slow the pace of new organizing. The North American Free Trade Agreement (NAFTA) in 1994, the normalization of trade with China in 2000, and other trade policies supported by multinational corporations accelerated the decline of the most union-dense industries in the private sector, manufacturing. After 2001, the country lost 42,400 factories in just eight years. The United States doesn't build much anymore; in 2017, the total value of our exports was one of the lowest in the world.

When I was growing up in the Midwest, the union was a symbol of strength: the union could make or break politicians; the union had the backs of men like Uncle Jimmy; and the "union guys" in the city were the tough guys. The international union fight song, "Solidarity Forever," has "The union makes us strong" as its refrain. At Nissan in Canton, the antiunion forces won in part by turning the union into a sign of weakness, a refuge for the "lazy." Messages linked the union with degrading stereotypes about black people, so that white workers wouldn't want any part of it. Even black workers might think they were too good to "need" a union.

At the worker center, I asked Melvin about how unions are perceived where he lives. "The people that we see, as soon as they see UAW, and even if you bring up union, they just think color. They just see color. They think that unions, period—not just UAW—they just think unions, period, are for lazy black people. . . . And a lot of 'em, even though they want the union, their racism, that hatred is keeping them from joining."

Johnny agreed with Melvin's assessment of his fellow white workers. "They get their southern mentality. . . . 'I ain't votin' [yes] because the blacks are votin' for it. If the blacks are for it, I'm against it.'"

I looked around the office, which included posters from various UAW Nissan rallies invoking the civil rights movement and the March on Washington. I wondered how the explicit embrace of civil rights imagery and language had played with the white co-workers they were trying to organize. It seemed like a catch-22: the majority of the plant was black, and the base of the worker organizing needed to be, too—so, invoking black struggle made sense. But particularly in the South, white workers might not see anything for themselves in a campaign redolent of the civil rights movement; at worst, the association could trigger the zero-sum reaction.

The word *union* itself seemed to be a dog whistle in the South, code for undeserving people of color who needed a union to compensate for some flaw in their character. As the workers spoke, I realized that it couldn't be a coincidence that, to this day, the region that is the least unionized, with the lowest state minimum wages and the weakest labor protections overall, was the one that had been built on slave labor—on a system that compensated the labor of black people at exactly zero.

UNIONS ARE FOR EQUAL GROUND

When I went back to my hotel after the first day of conversations with Nissan workers, I was dismayed and perplexed. I had assumed that white solidarity with black workers would be in the white workers' self-interest, but after listening to a day of stories about the ways that white workers were given special advantages at the plant, I wasn't so sure. Maybe the status quo—where being white actually did make it easier for you to get ahead, where a mostly white management could arbitrarily act to the benefit of those with whom they felt a kinship—was actually better for the average white worker than a union and its rules. I thought about Trent, a verbose prounion white guy still working on the line, because, as he said

proudly, he was too mouthy for white management to have promoted him to an easier job. But when describing his fellow white
workers, he had said: "The unions are for putting people on equal
ground. Some people see that as a threat to their society." As Earl
had said, "Even the white guys on the line, they felt they would
lose some power if we had a union. The view is, white people are in
charge, I'm in charge."

I realized that I had been naive to think that the benefits of the
union would be obvious to white workers. Having grown up in the
Midwest, I knew that the Nissan plant workers were getting a bad
deal compared to unionized autoworkers—lower pay, uncertain retirement, no job security, no way to bargain for better conditions at
all. But the white workers in Canton were still getting, or had the
promise of getting, a better deal than *someone*. The company was
able to redraw the lines of allegiance—not worker to worker, but
white to white—for the relatively low cost of a few perks. A white
worker starting a job on the line would quickly learn the unwrit-
ten racial rules. He'd see that he could get promoted to a "cushier"
job if he played his cards right, and that included not signing a
union card. No matter that nobody on the plant floor, no matter
how cushy their job, had a real pension or the right to bargain for
improvements at the plant. They could be satisfied with a slightly
better job that set them just above the black guys on the line, more
satisfied by a taste of status than they were hungry for a real pension, better health care, or better wages for everyone.

* * *

On my last morning in Canton, I had breakfast in my hotel's lobby with Chip Wells, the man who'd become a controversial figure at the plant in the final weeks before the vote on whether to unionize. He had been an outspoken white voice on the prounion organizing committee—so much so that he became the target of intimidation from antiunion people at the plant. He showed me a snapshot on his phone of his employee ID photo printed out as a poster in the security guards' room—someone had drawn a teardrop tattoo onto his left cheek and some kind of cross or swastika on his forehead. One of the people he worked alongside in the generally antiunion maintenance department (one of the better-paid departments) began to joke about Chip "gettin' hurt or fallin'." Eventually, Chip said he thought, "'Maybe he ain't joking,' you know? 'Cause he's from Natchez, and that's where they actually had [slave] auction blocks and stuff."

The pressure eventually got to him, and at a rally one Sunday, Chip donned an antiunion shirt, signaling to the cheers of white workers around him that he had switched sides. Chip told me that during the time he was "anti," as they called it, he was struck by the zero-sum mindset of the people on his team. "The idea's that if you uplift black people, you're downin' white people. It's like the world has a crab-in-a-barrel mentality. Every time somebody's gettin' on top, we gotta pull them down 'cause they might try to do us wrong or keep us down."

White workers who supported the union, like Trent and Johnny, told me that their view was different from that of most of their white peers because they saw their interests as the same as those of the black workers. In their telling, everybody would benefit from better health care, plant safety, pay raises, job security, retirement benefits, and a fair system for promotions to replace what they call the buddy buddy system, where who you hunt with matters more than your work ethic.

At the end of a long week in Mississippi, I boarded a small regional plane out of the state. As I sat looking over my notes, a grief I'd held at bay during all my conversations with those extraordinary everyday people grabbed at me, and I wept. What they wanted for themselves, their children, and their community—what they wanted even for the people in the plant who despised them—was a little more say over the decisions that shaped their lives. And they'd been defeated, by a powerful, profitable corporation and the very old zero-sum story.

THE SOLIDARITY DIVIDEND AT WORK

But there's another story woven through the history of worker struggle in America, of people refusing to fight alone and winning the Solidarity Dividend of better jobs, despite the odds. Over the past decade, that story gained a new chapter, written by some of the least-likely, lowest-paid workers in our economy. The movement began on November 29, 2012, when about two hundred fast-food workers rallied just outside Times Square, in the heart of Manhattan. They were hourly workers at the bottom of the pay scale, almost all brown and black, mostly young adults, often with children. They worked at Burger King, McDonald's, Subway, and

Sbarro, but they had either walked off the job or not gone in at all in order to attend an unprecedented one-day strike across the city. They chanted slogans like "One-two-three-four, time for you to pay more! Five-six-seven-eight, don't you dare retaliate!" Without a union's protection, they could have been fired upon their return to work, but they gained courage in numbers. Their demand? A raise from the minimum wage of $7.25 an hour to $15 an hour and a union. It was audacious.

Within a year, what would become the Fight for $15 had spread across the country.

Terrence Wise never thought that this would be his life at age forty-three. It's not that he was surprised to be working in fast food: his mother raised him on a Hardee's paycheck, so he grew up knowing that big chain restaurants offered hard but honest and always available work. Too many family bills to juggle caused Terrence to drop out of high school to work full-time, and in the twenty years since, he'd barely seen a raise. Even though he worked so many hours that he was always missing his three daughters, he hadn't been able to avoid a spell of homelessness. All that, though depressing, seemed pretty much the norm in America. What Terrence never expected, though, was that he'd find himself in the leadership of a global movement, speaking at the White House and testifying before the US Congress. Though he'd been an honors-track student and won awards for public speaking in high school, all that promise was far from his mind on the Sunday in 2012 when three people—two black, one white—walked into his Burger King and asked him to imagine more.

"It was a Domino's worker, a McDonald's worker, and a Subway worker," Terrence recalled to me with a smile in his voice. The three workers asked him: Do you think fast-food workers should earn a living wage, vacation, and health benefits? "Well, I hadn't seen a doctor—at that point, it'd been years, over a decade—so, yeah," he recalled telling the workers. "We deserve the opportunity for benefits, paid time off, sick days, things that we don't have." They told him they were organizing their fellow fast-food workers across the city. Terrence told them to count him in, and by the end of the day, he had signed up the six coworkers on his shift to join Stand Up KC (Kansas City), a group that would eventually join in the national Fight for $15.

Terrence got his first taste of collective action's power when he and his coworkers wrote up a petition and confronted the supervisor to demand simple safety improvements: stock up the first-aid kit, fix the broken wheels on the grease trap, replace the hoses that were leaking hot grease ("just simple things that we know billion-dollar corporations like McDonald's, Burger King, can afford")—and it worked. The first time he went out on a one-day walkout protest from his job at Burger King, he came back, and his boss gave him a dollar or so raise, when he had been refusing for years. "So, I've seen the power of coming together and organizing, and how it can make change. And I've definitely lived the life of when we were not organized . . . and how life just deteriorated over the years."

Part of what had kept the fast-food workers in Kansas City unorganized was a racial and cultural divide. Historically one of the country's most segregated cities along lines of black and white, Kansas City had also seen an increase in the Latinx population in the late 1990s, after NAFTA. Workers of different cultures didn't communicate much; language was a barrier in some instances, and there were rumors that Latinx managers were giving Latinx workers higher pay and sick days. Getting workers out of the stores, into each other's homes, and sharing their stories helped dispel these myths. From the beginning, Stand Up KC named racism as a common enemy. Its first printed banner read: UNITED AGAINST RACISM—GOOD JOBS FOR ALL.

The message has resonated with Terrence. "We've got to build a multiracial movement, a different kind of social justice movement for the [twenty-first] century. And we've got to talk about it, multiracial organizing and how to build the movement, you know?

"We've got to have a new vision for America. We're building the Fight for $15 and a union movement, and we've got to have a new identity for the working class. What do we do every day in this country? All of us get up and go to work. We make this country run. And now, more than ever, workers are producing more wealth than we've received, you know? We're being exploited across the board," he told me over the phone, and I could just picture him bringing a crowd to its feet.

I thought back to Canton; the UAW's message about race had invoked civil rights for black workers, but the fast-food message explicitly included white people in the coalition and named division, not just racial oppression, as a common enemy. That story helped transform the way Bridget Hughes saw the world.

Bridget is a white woman whose Irish ancestry shows up in her reddish hair and whose Missouri accent is slight but unmistakable to those who know how to listen for it. She has three children and has worked in fast food for over a decade. Like Terrence, she was an honors student with college potential, but she had to drop out to support her family when her mother got sick. When Bridget was first approached by a coworker at Wendy's about joining Stand Up KC, she was skeptical, to say the least. "I didn't think that things in my life would ever change. They weren't going to give fifteen dollars to a fast-food worker—that was just insane to me." But she went to the first meeting anyway. When a Latinx woman rose and described her life—three children in a two-bedroom apartment with plumbing issues, the feeling of being "trapped in a life where she didn't have any opportunity to do anything better"—Bridget was moved.

"I was really able to see myself in her. And at that point, I decided that the only way we was gonna fix it was if all of us came together. Whether we were white, brown, black. It didn't matter." For Bridget to see herself in a Latinx worker was a breakthrough. She admitted, "When I first joined the movement, I had been fed this whole line of 'These immigrant workers are coming over here and stealing our jobs . . . not paying taxes, committing crimes, and causing problems.' [It was] other white people in my family who believe these kind of racist ideas. You know, us against them." But she said she saw her bosses at Wendy's target Latinx workers, falsely promising them a raise if they didn't join the strikes. "They knew that if our Latino workers joined with our black and white workers, that we'd have our strength in numbers, and that we was gonna win."

Since joining Stand Up KC, Bridget's worldview has changed. "In order for all of us to come up, it's not a matter of me coming up and them staying down. It's the matter of, in order for me to come up, they have to come up, too—because we have to come up together. Because honestly, as long as we're divided, we're conquered. The only way that we're going to succeed is together." And they did succeed: Stand Up KC lobbied the city council to raise the local minimum wage to $13 an hour. (Almost immediately, the Republican state legislature passed a law forbidding any municipality from requiring a wage higher than the state's $7.70, a move that would be replicated by Republican legislatures across the country.)

This fight for decent pay has, like many labor struggles before it, exposed the fact that workers of color suffer the most acute economic injustices, but most of the people harmed in a wage structure built on racism are white. And like every truly successful labor movement, it has found its reach and its strength because of cross-racial solidarity.

What was the difference between the worker struggle at Nissan in Mississippi and the one at fast-food chains in Kansas City? Those fighting for $15 undoubtedly had less to lose—the Legacy Nissan workers who could vote made more than twice what fast-food workers were paid and, in a way, could "free-ride" on a wage floor lifted by decades of labor organizing in Detroit. But the campaigns' strategies were also different. By inviting white workers to see how the powerful profited from selling them a racist story that cost everybody ("whether brown, black or white," as workers so often said), the Fight for $15 had managed to win the support of whites as well.

By almost every financial measure, the Fight for $15 has been a success, creating a Solidarity Dividend that reversed a trend of two generations of stagnant and declining wages for the lowest-paid workers. Many of the workers who rallied on that first day in 2012 near Times Square went on to testify at the New York State Capitol in 2016, when they won a statewide $15 minimum wage. So, too, did workers in states including California, Connecticut, Illinois, Maryland, Massachusetts, and New Jersey, and in Washington, DC, as well as cities that include Flagstaff, Arizona; the Twin Cities; and Seattle, all of which have raised, or committed to raising, wages to $15 an hour. In addition to these policy wins, workers won private wage increases at giant employers including Walmart, Bank of America, McDonald's (which also announced it would stop lobbying against minimum wage increases), and Amazon. It turns out that more money in people's pockets is not just good for rich people when it comes to tax cuts—and that employers could have afforded it all along. There was no drop in employment in places with wage increases, and in fact, many places have found the opposite.

The more elusive goal for the Fight for $15 and a union has been the last part: the union. With high turnover and hundreds of shops per city, organizing workers restaurant by restaurant might take decades. The key to unionization of the thousands of franchises is for the law to recognize that umbrella corporations like McDonald's are joint employers with the franchise owners, as they set virtually all the terms of business. The Service Employees International Union (SEIU) made this case before the courts, the National Labor Relations Board agreed with them in 2015, and it looked like American fast-food workers were going to join their counterparts in many European countries in having a way to bargain for higher wages and benefits. But one of the first moves from the Trump administration was to reverse the Obama NLRB decision on franchise joint employment.

The majority of workers in American fast food come from the same white, working-class pool of voters who went overwhelmingly for Trump, a man whose campaign was dominated by promises to fight for the (white) working class and punish immigrants. When I spoke with her after the 2016 election, Bridget Hughes connected Trump's election to the urgency of Stand Up KC's cross-racial organizing: "Kind of the whole point of this movement is for white workers to understand that racism affects white workers as well. Because it keeps us divided from our black and our brown brothers and sisters. So, we need to understand that as white workers, we, too, need to stand up and fight against racism."

As I was wrapping up my last visit to the worker center in Canton, Mississippi, I took the time to walk around the space. An unadorned storefront had been transformed with posters, printed and hand-drawn; photos from rallies; and pictures of workers' kids.

People came in for coffee and company after their overnight shifts ended at dawn, and they'd come in before work to gear up for the long shift ahead. I recalled something Chip had said that morning as I got ready to leave our breakfast. First, he wanted me to know that despite his visible defection in the last weeks, he'd stayed true when the time came: "I got in that booth, and it was very liberating to vote yes." Second, even though he was afraid he wouldn't be welcome anymore at the worker center, he needed me to know about the solidarity he felt there. "I felt a sense of belonging, of love, of togetherness, friendship," he said, with emotion in his voice. "We went through a lot together, and did a lot together, and accomplished a lot. . . . I loved it. I loved goin' over there. . . . It was, I guess, utopia without havin' utopia."

CHAPTER 6

NEVER A REAL DEMOCRACY

"**I** BELIEVE IF YOU CAN'T HAVE YOUR FUNDAMENTAL RIGHT OF voting, what do you have? You don't have nothin'." These words could have been spoken by a black person during the march from Selma to Montgomery for voting rights in 1965, but they were spoken in 2017 by a middle-aged white Ohioan named Larry Harmon. A navy veteran and software engineer, Larry has a round face, a salt-and-pepper beard, and eyebrows that are quick to flight when he's incredulous about something—which he was often as Demos, whose name means "the people of a nation" and is the root word of *democracy,* and the ACLU represented him in a case that went all the way to the US Supreme Court. It was a case that aimed to strike down a process that had imperiled Larry's right to vote, a right he'd be the first to admit that he, unlike his black fellow citizens, never thought he'd have to fight for.

Democracy is a secular religion in America; faith in it unites us. Even when we are critical of our politics, we wouldn't trade our form of government for any other, and we have even gone to war to defend it from competition with rival systems. Yet our sacred system allows a Larry Harmon to lose his opportunity for self-governance as easily as one lets a postcard fall in with the grocery circulars and wind up in the trash.

The truth is, we have never had a real democracy in America. The framers of the Constitution broke with a European tradition of monarchy and aspired to a revolutionary vision of self-governance, yet they compromised their own ideals from the start. The framers left holes in the bedrock of our democracy from the outset, in order to leave room for slavery. Since then, in the interest of racial subjugation, America has repeatedly attacked its own foundations.

Possibly the most consequential of the founding racist distortions in our democracy was the creation of the Electoral College in lieu of direct election of the president. James Madison believed that direct election would be the most democratic, but to secure slave states' ratification of the Constitution, he devised the Electoral College as a compromise to give those states an advantage. As a result, the US apportions presidential electoral votes to states based on their number of House and Senate members. With the South's House delegations stacked by the Constitution's Three-Fifths Compromise—Northern states having granted Southern states the right to count three-fifths of their enslaved population in determining the states' voting power in Congress and the Electoral College—the region had thirteen extra electors in the country's first elections and Virginia was able to boost its sons to win eight of the first nine presidential contests. The three-fifths clause became moot after Emancipation and black male suffrage at the end of the Civil War, but the Electoral College's distortions remain. An Electoral College built to protect slavery has sent two recent candidates to the White House, George W. Bush and Donald J. Trump, who both lost the popular vote. The Electoral College still overrepresents white people, but in an interesting parallel to the free/slave tilt from the original Constitution, not all white people benefit. The advantage accrues to white people who live in whiter, less-populated states; white people who live in larger states that look more like America are the ones underrepresented today.

FREEDOM GAINED, VOTE DENIED

In the years after the Civil War and the emancipation of enslaved people, federal troops traveled across the South registering seven hundred thousand recently freed black men. The white backlash to black suffrage was immediate, and not just by elites who saw their political privilege threatened. In Colfax, Louisiana, for example, when a pro-Reconstruction candidate supported by black voters won a fiercely contested gubernatorial race in 1872; the following spring, a mob of armed white men attacked the courthouse where the certification of the election had been held, killing about one hundred black people who were trying to defend the building, and setting the courthouse on fire. The white citizens murdered their neighbors and burned the edifice of their own government rather than submit to a multiracial democracy.

* * *

The one hundred years of American history following Reconstruction were shaped by relentless assaults on the right of black and Indigenous Americans to vote and by elite efforts to prevent class-based interracial resistance. Because the Constitution's Fifteenth Amendment barred states from denying the right to vote based on color, class served as a proxy. The Reconstruction era saw movements of impoverished white farmers making common cause with black freedmen in political parties and populist alliances sometimes known as Fusion. Their aim was to break the grip the plantation oligarchy had on government and the economy, provide interest rate relief to debtors, raise taxes for public works, and resist railroad land grabs. The ruling class fought against the cross-racial populists with a campaign for "white supremacy," promising material and other advantages to whites who broke with blacks—and violent intimidation to those who didn't.

When they won, the white supremacists attacked the franchise first. In 1890, unsure that one barrier to the ballot would suffice to control growing Reconstruction-era black political power, Mississippi implemented literacy tests, new registration rules, standards for "good character," poll taxes, and more. Other states soon created similar laws, and poor white voters were caught up in the dragnet. For instance, poll taxes, usually in the range of $1 to $2 ($2 in 1890 being almost $57 in today's money), required cash of poor white, black, and Indigenous people who were often sharecroppers with little cash to their names. In some places, grandfather clauses exempted whites whose grandfathers could vote before the war; in others, candidates or party officials would pay white voters' taxes for them in exchange for their loyalty. But in many places, the poll tax continued to work almost as effectively to disenfranchise poor white people as it did black people, and the result was a slow death of civic life. After several Southern states adopted the menu of voter suppression tactics, turnout of eligible white voters throughout the region plummeted. In the presidential election of 1944, when national turnout averaged 69 percent, the poll tax states managed a scant 18 percent.

Some of the voter manipulation tactics of the post–Civil War era remain in full force today. All of them disproportionately impact people of color but diminish our entire system of self-governance. The requirement that we register to vote at all before Election Day did not become common until after the Civil War, when black people had their first chance at the franchise. Throughout its history, writes legal scholar Daniel P. Tokaji, "voter registration has thus been a means not only of promoting election integrity, but also of impeding eligible citizens' access to the ballot." Today, the burdensome and confusing registration process is particularly onerous on people who move frequently (young people, people of color, and low-income people) or who may not know about lower-profile, off-cycle election dates before the registration deadlines, which are as much as thirty days before the election in some states. One of the top barriers to voting, the registration requirement kept nearly 20 percent of eligible voters from the polls in 2016.

Over six million Americans are prohibited from voting as a

by-product of the racist system of mass incarceration. (The only states that allow people with felony convictions to vote even while they're in prison are Maine and Vermont, the two whitest states in the nation.) The disenfranchisement laws, combined with discriminatory policing and sentencing, hit their target and today ensnare one in thirteen African American voters. But their reach is wider than their aim: one in fifty-six non-black voters is impacted as well. In Florida, voters in 2018 overturned the state's lifetime disenfranchisement of people with felony convictions by ballot measure, enabling more than a million people to regain their voting rights—the majority of whom are white.

Coral Nichols is a white woman in her early forties from Largo, Florida, and is among the hundreds of thousands of white Floridians denied the right to vote under the state's Reconstruction-era felony disenfranchisement law. While she was still on probation, Coral started volunteering with the Florida Rights Restoration Coalition (FRRC)—"because we've served our time, and we should be given the opportunity to belong," she explained to me. Coral went door to door in her county encouraging local citizens to do what she could not—vote on a ballot initiative to restore voting rights to people like her. Coral could tell that a lot of people she spoke to had a preconceived notion about people with felony convictions: "They think that most felons are monsters. They don't see the depth of a personal story, which is why I think that stories are so important." Race played a role, too—and that's why Coral always chose to canvass alongside an African American "brother or sister," as she put it. "It was important that we were united together.

When we encountered any type of stereotype, what could break the stereotype was what was standing in front of them." Amendment 4 passed with 65 percent of the vote on November 6, 2018, and on April 19, 2019, Coral finally got released from the ten years of probation that followed her incarceration and was free to register to vote.

In reaction to Amendment 4, Florida's Republican governor and legislature passed a state law that required people with a felony history to pay all outstanding fines and fees before voting. This move—redolent of the poll tax—is particularly troubling in Florida, where it is nearly impossible for returning citizens to find out what the state thinks they owe and where "there is no database . . . to be able to check all the different court costs that might be outstanding," as one county supervisor of elections testified. The restrictive new law was challenged in court but upheld by a federal appeals court in September 2020. Coral is among approximately eighty-five thousand returning citizens who registered to vote before the new restrictive law went into effect and who must prove they have paid up before they can vote.

HURDLES AND TRAPS

All of these laws to limit voting have their effect, shrinking the power of American democracy. Think about it: today, no politician worries that their position in a representative government is illegitimate even if only a minority of citizens votes in their election. They should. What does it mean when the officials who set policy in our name are elected by so few of us? We shouldn't take these low standards for granted. Our election system is full of unnecessary hurdles and traps—some set by malice and some by negligence—but I would argue that all are a product of the same basic tolerance for a compromised republic that was established at our founding, in the interest of racial slavery. Countries less boastful of their democracies do much better. In Australia, voting is mandatory, and nearly 97 percent of Australians are registered, compared to about 70 percent registration and 61 percent voting in the United States. Canada and Germany don't make voting compulsory, but their registration rates are about 93 and 91 percent, respectively.

America's fifty states, and even counties within them, confuse and discourage voters with an archaic patchwork of varying laws, rules, and practices. In some states, you can go to the polls on Election Day and sign up as you vote. In others, you have to register thirty days before an election, a deadline you're likely to know only if you've missed it. In some states—a growing number since the COVID-19 pandemic—you can vote at home and mail in your ballot, while in others, you have to provide an excuse for why you could not go in person. Not surprisingly, Americans at all educational levels are deeply uncertain about their own states' election laws. In states that prohibit early voting, only 15 percent of residents are aware of this restriction. In states that allow same-day registration, only a quarter of its residents know it. Around half of Americans are unsure whether their state permits them to vote if they have unpaid utility bills or traffic tickets—prohibitions that no states have adopted (yet).

To see what US democracy would be like without the distorting factor of racism, we can look to the states that make it easiest to vote, which are some of the whitest. Oregon, for example, was judged the easiest state in which to vote by a comprehensive study. In Oregon, everyone votes by mailing in a ballot, and Oregon was the first state in the nation to adopt automatic voter registration (AVR), which means that rather than making voters figure out how, when, and where to register, Oregon uses information the state already has, for instance from the DMV, to add eligible voters to the rolls. North Dakota, another largely white state, boasts of being the only state without any requirement of voter registration. Until a 2018 voter ID law aimed at Indigenous North Dakotans, you could simply have a poll worker vouch for you at the polling place. Mississippi, the state with the highest percentage of black citizens, is dead last of the fifty states in terms of ease of voting.

A NEW WAVE OF VOTER SUPPRESSION

For most of America's history, voter suppression was strongest in the Jim Crow states where the black population threatened white political control. But after the election of the first African American president, every state became a potential threat to white control. A new wave of voter suppression, funded by a coterie of right-wing billionaires, crashed into states like Florida, North Carolina, Ohio, and Wisconsin—swing states that could turn a presidential election.

These same billionaires funded a lawsuit, *Shelby County v. Holder,* to bring a challenge to the Voting Rights Act's most powerful pro-vision. Decided by a 5–4 majority at the beginning of President Obama's second term, *Shelby County v. Holder* lifted the federal government's protection from citizens in states and counties with long records of discriminatory voting procedures. Immediately across the country, Republican legislatures felt free to restrict vot-ing rights. North Carolina legislators imposed a photo ID law that a court found "target[ed] African Americans with almost surgical precision," because it was based on research that pinpointed the kinds of identification to which white people had greater access and then allowed only those forms of ID. Texas introduced a voter ID law that essentially let the state design its own electorate, re-quiring photo IDs that over half a million eligible voters lacked and specifying what kinds of IDs would be permitted (gun per-mits, 80 percent of which are owned by white Texans) and denied (college IDs, in a state where more than 50 percent of students are people of color). Alabama demanded photo IDs from voters, such as a driver's license, and within a year, it closed thirty-one driver's license offices, including in eight out of ten of the most populous black counties. Between the 2013 *Shelby* decision and the 2018 election, twenty-three states raised new barriers to voting. Al-though about 11 percent of the US population (disproportionately low-income people, seniors, and people of color) do not have ac-cess to photo IDs, by 2020, six states still demanded them in order for people to vote, and an additional twenty-six states made voting much easier if you had an ID.

These policies were targeted primarily to disadvantage people of color, but such broad brooms have swept large numbers of white people into the democratic margins as well. In general, about 5 percent of white people in the United States lack a photo ID. Within certain portions of the white population, however, the numbers increase: 19 percent of white people with household incomes below $25,000 have neither a driver's license nor a passport. The same is true of 20 percent of white people ages seventeen to twenty. Of the fifty thousand already-registered Alabama voters estimated to lack proper photo ID to vote in 2016, more than half were white.

Antivoting lawmakers perhaps weren't intending to make it harder for married white women to vote, but that's exactly what they did by requiring an exact name match across all forms of identification in many states in recent years. Birth certificates list people's original surnames, but if they change their names upon marriage, their more recent forms of ID usually show their married names. Sandra Watts is a married white judge in the state of Texas who was forced to use a provisional ballot in 2013 under the state's voter ID law. She was outraged at the imposition: "Why would I want to vote provisional ballot when I've been voting regular ballot for the last forty-nine years?" Like many women, she included her maiden name as her middle name when she took her husband's last name—and that's what her driver's license showed. But on the voter rolls, her middle name was the one her parents gave her at birth, which she no longer used. And just like that, she lost her vote—all because of a law intended to suppress people like Judge Watts's fellow Texan Anthony Settles, a black septuagenarian and retired engineer.

Anthony Settles was in possession of his Social Security card, an expired Texas identification card, and his old University of Houston student ID, but he couldn't get a new photo ID to vote in 2016 because his mother had changed his name when she re-married in 1964. Several lawyers tried to help him track down the name-change certificate in courthouses, to no avail; his only re-course was to go to court for a new one, at a cost of $250. Elderly, rural, and low-income voters are more likely not to have birth cer-tificates or to have documents containing clerical errors. Hargie Randell, a legally blind black Texan who couldn't drive but who had a current voter registration card used before the new Texas law, had to arrange for people to drive him to the Department of Public Safety office three times, and once to the county clerk's office an hour away, only to end up with a birth certificate that spelled his name wrong by one letter. Our unequal democracy is like so much of modern-day structural racism: it harms people of color dispro-portionately but doesn't spare nonwealthy white people; it may be hard to assign racist intent, but it's easy to find the racist impacts.

PURGING VOTERS

Possibly the most insidious antivoting innovation to appear after the Obama election was the purge of unwitting voters already reg-istered to vote. In 2015, Larry Harmon's elected secretary of state, Jon Husted, used a purge process to eliminate two hundred thou-sand registered Ohio voters from the rolls in the state's twenty most populous counties, all in the name of list maintenance to prevent voter fraud. As in most states, these high-population counties were also the ones whose residents were most likely to be people of color and to vote Democratic.

Here's how the purge process worked. If an Ohio voter failed to vote during a two-year period—say, he voted in the presidential election but sat out the midterms—the state mailed the voter a post-card to verify his address. If the voter didn't return the postcard, the state launched a process that, unless the person cast a ballot within the next four years, would result in his name being purged from the rolls—he was no longer considered a valid voter in the state. There are a number of problems with this approach, starting with the fact that in the United States, voting is not a use-it-or-lose-it right. What's more, as Secretary Husted knew perfectly well, the vast majority of people who receive these address-verification postcards in the mail do not return them. In 2012, Ohio went to the trouble and expense of sending out 1.5 million address-verification notices to people who hadn't voted in 2011—out of a total of only 7.7 million registered voters. Presuming a change in registration for almost one out of every five registered voters is a remarkably wasteful effort, given that only about three out of every one hundred people move out of a registrar's jurisdiction in any given year.

Of the 1.5 million postcard recipients, 1.2 million never responded. This should have been a clue that something was wrong with the state's notification process, not with the voters. Or perhaps the process was working precisely as intended: people of color, renters, and young people are significantly less likely to respond to official mail than are white people, homeowners, and older people, as the Census Bureau had discovered.

"I've lived in Ohio my entire life," explained Larry Harmon, "except for when I served in the navy, and even then, I paid Ohio taxes." Yet, in 2015, Larry felt like he'd been disappeared in the eyes of the state. "When I went to vote, I went into the hall and I looked up my name, and I looked and I looked, but I didn't see my name.

"While I was at work on my lunch hour, I tried to google to see, did I do something wrong? . . . I didn't quite understand why I wouldn't be on the list; I'd voted there before." Then he ran across information on Ohio's purge of inactive voters. "I didn't think I was required to vote in every election!" Larry said, incredulity in his voice.

He had been voting since 1976, mostly in presidential elections. His reasons for skipping the 2012 election were, like those of so many Americans, both personal and political: a combination of a lack of inspiration and the pressures of real life. "I think I went through a period after my mother's death that I wasn't interested in voting, and I didn't think it did a whole lot of good, so I didn't vote for one presidential election and, they told me, one midterm election."

But in 2015, Larry was closely following an issue that he knew would be on the ballot—a proposal to legalize marijuana but to concentrate the industry in a few corporate hands. He was opposed to the idea and was eager to have his say. And the more Larry thought about being denied the opportunity to vote, the more upset he became.

"I thought, 'Well, jeez. You know, I pay my taxes every year, and I pay my property taxes, and I register my car.' So, the state had to know I'm still a voter. Why should we fight for the country if they're gonna be taking away my rights? I mean, I'm a veteran, my father's a veteran, my grandfather's a veteran. Now they aren't giving me my right to vote, the most fundamental right I have?"

Lawyers at my organization learned of Ohio's singularly aggressive purging practice—no other state initiated a purge process after just one missed federal election—and concluded that it violated federal law, the National Voter Registration Act of 1993. Most commonly known as the motor voter law because it made registration more available at DMVs and other government offices, the law also bars states from a number of burdensome voter registration practices, including purging registered voters for not voting. In early 2016, Demos took Ohio to court, and over the next two years battled the case all the way up to the Supreme Court.

On January 10, 2018, I was in Washington, DC, to watch the oral arguments before the Supreme Court for the case, which was now called *Husted v. A. Philip Randolph Institute* (APRI). The early morning was chilly as I walked to the court building with my colleague Stuart Naifeh, who had argued the case successfully in the lower court. As we climbed the wide stone steps, I looked up at the words inscribed in marble above the court's columns: EQUAL JUSTICE UNDER THE LAW. I couldn't help contrasting those stirring words with the mess Ohio had made of its voting system. A narrow 5–4 vote on the Supreme Court ruled against us in the case.

Despite our contemporary reverence for the idea of equality under the law, the truth is the Constitution wasn't written with an affirmative right to vote for all citizens. It's always been a power struggle to create a representative electorate, and currently, the forces against equality have the upper hand.

Voter suppression, an age-old racist tactic, has been reanimated in recent years by subtly anti-black and anti-brown propaganda, but is now useful against a broad base of white people who could be in a multiracial coalition with people of color. I spoke to a democracy historian named Nancy MacLean about the impacts of new voting barriers. "The voter suppression legislation in many cases, certainly in [my state of] North Carolina, didn't only aim at African Americans. It also aimed in particular at young people. In my state, they took pains to eliminate a program that led to the automatic registration of high school students. . . . They took aim at early voting, which tends to be something that many young people also use. And frankly, many white people prefer, too. . . . They also moved polling sites away from campuses," she told me.

THE SOLIDARITY DIVIDEND OF DEMOCRACY

The fear that drives the violence and mendacity of American voter suppression is rooted in a zero-sum vision of democracy: either I have the power and the spoils, or you do. But I take heart in remembering that the civil rights–era liberation of the African American vote in the South offered a Solidarity Dividend for white people as well. The elimination of the poll tax in particular freed up the political participation of lower-income white voters. Indeed, white voters in Georgia and Virginia had challenged the poll tax requirement, but the courts upheld it in 1937 and 1951. After the civil rights movement knocked down voting barriers, white as well as black registration and turnout rates rose in former Jim Crow states. And a fuller democracy meant more than just a larger number of ballots; it meant a more responsive government for the people who hadn't been wealthy enough to have influence before.

"When you talk about the effects of the Voting Rights Act and political participation, just going to the ballot box and casting your vote is only one step," economist Gavin Wright told me. He's the author of *Sharing the Prize*, which details the economic benefits the civil rights movement brought to the entire South, whites included. "What the black political leadership got, and economic leadership, was a seat at the table." With that seat, they won investments in public infrastructure, including hospitals, roads, schools, and libraries that had been starved when one-party rule allowed only the Southern aristocracy to set the rules. More voters of all races meant more competitive elections; for the first time since the end of Reconstruction, a white-supremacy campaign wasn't enough. Candidates had to promise to deliver something of value to Southern families, white and black. In *Sharing the Prize*, Wright writes that "after the Voting Rights Act . . . southern . . . gubernatorial campaigns increasingly featured nonracial themes of economic development and education."

Research shows that states with higher levels of participation by working-class citizens have fairer economic policies and healthier families. That's the Solidarity Dividend that we can unlock through a truly representative, multiracial democracy.

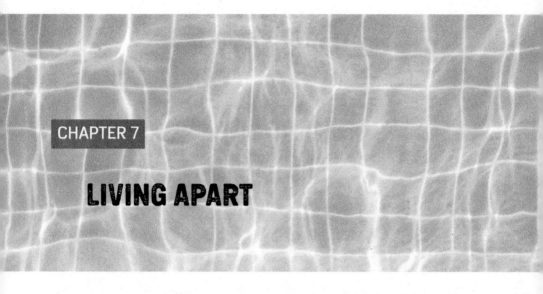

CHAPTER 7

LIVING APART

WHITE PEOPLE ARE THE MOST SEGREGATED PEOPLE IN America.

That's a different way to think about what has perennially been an issue cast with the opposite die: people of color are those who are segregated, because the white majority separates out the black minority, excludes the Chinese, forces Indigenous Americans onto reservations, expels the Latinx. Segregation is a problem for those on the outside because what is good is reserved for those within. While that has historically been materially true, as government subsidies nurtured wealth inside white spaces and suppressed and stripped wealth outside, I wanted to investigate the damage done to all of us, including white people, by the persistence of segregation. The typical white person lives in a neighborhood that is at least 75 percent white. In today's increasingly multiracial society, where white people value diversity but rarely live it, there are costs—financial, developmental, even physical—to continuing to segregate as we do. Marisa Novara, a Chicago housing official, put it this way: "I think as a field, we use the word *segregation* incorrectly. I think we tend to use it as if it's a synonym for places that are low-income, where black and brown people live. And we ignore all of the places that are majority white, that are exclusive enclaves, as if those are not segregated as well."

Few people today understand the extent to which governments at every level forced Americans to live apart throughout our history. Our governments not only imposed color restrictions on where people could live and work, but also on where we could shop and buy gas, watch movies, drink water, enter buildings, and walk on the sidewalk. The obsession with which America drew the color line was all-consuming and absurd. And contrary to our collective memory, segregation didn't originate in the South; nor was it confined to the Jim Crow states. Segregation was first developed in the Northern states before the Civil War. Boston had a "Nigger Hill" and "New Guinea." Moving west: territories like Illinois and Oregon limited or barred free black people entirely in the first half of the 1800s. In the South, white dependence on black labor, and white need for physical control and access to black bodies, required proximity, the opposite of segregation. The economic imperative set the terms of the racial understanding; in the South, blacks were seen as inferior and servile but needed to be close. In the North, black people were job competition, therefore seen as dangerous, stricken with a poverty that could be infectious.

The Reconstruction reforms after the Civil War should have ended segregation. Congress passed a broad Civil Rights Act in 1875, banning discrimination in public accommodations. During Reconstruction, many southern cities had "salt-and-pepper" integration, in which black and white people lived in the same neighborhoods and even dined in the same restaurants. Multiracial working-class political alliances formed in North Carolina, Alabama, and Virginia. As it did after Bacon's Rebellion, though, the wealthy white power structure reacted to the threat of class solidarity by creating new rules to promote white supremacy. This time, they reasoned that everyday physical separation would be the most powerful way to ensure the allegiance of the white masses to race over class.

In 1883, the US Supreme Court struck down America's first Civil Rights Act, and the Black Codes of Jim Crow took hold, with mirrors in the North. In the words of the preeminent historian of the South, C. Vann Woodward, "Jim Crow laws put the authority of the state or city in the voice of the street-car conductor, the railway brakeman, the bus driver, the theater usher, and also into the voice of the hoodlum of the public parks and playgrounds. They gave free rein and the majesty of the law to mass aggressions that might otherwise have been curbed, blunted or deflected." Any white person was now deputized to enforce the exclusion of black people from white space, a terrible power that led to decades of sadistic violence against black men, women, and children.

For the next eighty years, segregation dispossessed Native Americans, Latinx, Asian Americans, and black Americans of land and often life. No governments in modern history save apartheid South Africa and Nazi Germany have segregated as well as the United States has, with precision and under the color of law. (And even then, both the Third Reich and the Afrikaner government looked to America's laws to create their systems.) US government financing required home developers and landlords to put racially restrictive covenants (agreements to sell only to white people) in their housing contracts. And as we've already seen, the federal government supported housing segregation through redlining and other banking practices, the result of which was that the two investments that created the housing market that has been a cornerstone of building wealth in American families, the thirty-year mortgage and the federal government's willingness to guarantee banks' issuance of those loans, were made on a whites-only basis and under conditions of segregation.

Even after the Supreme Court ruled in 1948 that governments could no longer enforce racial covenants in housing, the government continued to discriminate under the pretext of credit risk. Planners for the Interstate Highway System designated black and brown areas as undesirable and either destroyed them to make way for highways or located highways in ways that separated the neighborhoods from job-rich areas. The effects of these policy decisions are no more behind us than the houses we live in.

Instead of whites-only clauses in rental advertisements and color-coded maps, today's segregation is driven by less obviously racially targeted policies. I've often wondered how our suburbs became so homogenous, with such similar house sizes and types. It turns out that, like so much of how we live, it was no accident: after the Supreme Court invalidated city ordinances banning black people from buying property in white neighborhoods in 1917, over a thousand communities rushed to adopt "exclusionary zoning" laws to restrict the types of housing that most black people could afford to buy, especially without access to subsidized mortgages (such as units in apartment buildings or two-family homes). These rules remain today, an invisible layer of exclusion laid across 75 percent of the residential map in most American cities, effectively banning working-class and many middle-income people from renting or buying there. Exclusionary zoning rules limit the number of units constructed per acre; they can outright ban apartment buildings; they can even deem that a single-family house has to be big enough to preserve a neighborhood's "aesthetic uniformity." The effect is that they keep land supply short, house prices high, and multifamily apartment buildings out. In 1977, the Supreme Court failed to recognize that these rules were racial bans recast in class terms, and the impact on integration—not to mention housing affordability for millions of struggling white families—has been devastating.

Today, the crisis surrounding housing affordability in the United States is reaching a fever pitch: the majority of people in the one hundred largest US cities are now renters, and the majority of those renters spend more than half their income on rent. Homeownership rates are falling for many Americans as costs continue to increase, construction productivity continues to decline, and incomes don't keep pace. Nationwide, the typical home costs more than 4.2 times the typical household income; in 1970, the same ratio was 1.7. One solution many cities are investigating or implementing is an increase in the housing supply by limiting or eradicating single-family zoning. While the net effect of increasing housing supply doesn't always lead automatically to greater affordability without additional policy changes, the lasting legacy of the racism designed into American property markets did increase costs for all Americans.

A CHILDHOOD IN BLACK AND WHITE

I was born on the South Side of Chicago, in a neighborhood that is still a black working middle-class community, full of teachers and other public servants who found doors open in government that were closed in the private sector. There were also lots of owners of small businesses with an ethos that they'd rather make their own way than be "last hired, first fired," as the saying goes, in a white person's shop. The apartment where I was born is in a four-story brick building that my great-grandmother Flossie McGhee bought on a "land sale contract," one of the notorious high-interest contracts whites sold to black home buyers lacking access to mortgages because of redlining and bank discrimination. (In the 1960s, 85 percent of black homeowners bought on contract.) When you bought on contract, you built no equity until the end and could be evicted and lose everything if you missed a single payment. Against all odds, Grandma Flossie kept the payments coming with money she made by combining jobs as a nanny to white families with a lucky streak with the numbers, a sort of underground lottery. In our neighborhood of Chatham/Avalon, as far as I can recall and census data can confirm, there were no white people within a fifteen-block radius of us. Chicago is one of the most segregated cities in America, by design. Before the 1948 racial covenant Supreme Court decision, 80 percent of the city of Chicago carried racial covenants banning black people from living in most neighborhoods, a percentage that was similar in other large cities around the country, including Los Angeles.

A few times a week after school, I would visit my paternal grandparents, Earl and Marcia McGhee, a Chicago police officer and a Chicago public schools social worker. They lived on the other side of the "L," in a neighborhood known as Pill Hill because of all the single-family houses belonging to doctors from the neighboring hospital. Over there, it was the picture of success in brick and concrete: houses with manicured lawns, single-car garages, and monogrammed awnings over the doorsteps. But it was almost all-black, too; a few Jewish families hung on into the 1970s, but there were none on my grandparents' block when I was a kid. It was our own American Dream, hard-won and, for many who remember its glory days, almost utopian.

I asked my grandma Marcia about what the segregated South Side was like in those days. "We had a common history, all of us: parents who came up from terror and sharecropping to . . ." She laughed. "To deeds and degrees. In just one generation. And nobody gave us a thing. They were always trying to take, in fact. So, you'd walk down the street and see the new car in the driveway, the kids in the yard, and everybody was happy for each other's success, and you knew everybody'd be there for each other when you were down."

I never knew why the South Side where I grew up was so black, or that it hadn't always been. In the 1950s, Chatham's population was over 90 percent white. Ten years later, it was more than 60 percent black. By the time I was born there, in 1980, the population had been over 90 percent African American for a decade. But when I left home in middle school for an almost entirely all-white boarding school in rural Massachusetts, I learned two things about where I came from. The first was that the thickness of my black community—close-knit, represented in civic institutions, and economically dynamic—was rare. In Boston, black meant poor in a way I simply had never realized. The everyday sight of black doctors and managers (particularly native-born) was a rarity in that old-money city where black political power had never gained a hold and where negative stereotypes of blackness filled in the space. Second, I learned that although we knew about white people even if we didn't live with them—they were coworkers, school administrators, and of course, every image on-screen—segregation meant that white people didn't know much about us at all.

For all the ways that segregation is aimed at limiting the choices of people of color, it's white people who are ultimately isolated. In a survey taken during the uprisings in Ferguson, Missouri, after the police killing of Michael Brown, an unarmed black teenager, the majority of white Americans said they regularly came in contact with only "a few" African Americans, and a 2019 poll reported that 21 percent "seldom or never" interacted with any people of color at all. In 2016, three-quarters of white people reported that their social network was entirely white.

This white isolation continues amid rising racial and ethnic diversity in America, though few white people say they want it to—in fact, quite the opposite. Diversity has become a commonly accepted "good" despite its elusiveness; people seem to know that the more you interact with people who are different from you, the more commonalities you see and the less they seem like "the other." Research repeatedly bears this out. Take, for example, a meta-analysis that examined 515 studies conducted in 38 countries from the 1940s through 2000, which encompassed responses from 250,000 people. The social psychologist Linda Tropp explained the findings of this research in 2014, when she testified before the New York City Council in a hearing about the city's school system, the most segregated in the United States. "Approximately ninety-four percent of the cases in our analysis show a relationship such that greater contact is associated with lower prejudice." What's more, she said, "contact reduces our anxiety in relation to other groups and enhances our ability to empathize with other groups."

This is the strange paradox of white attitudes toward integration: in the course of two generations and one lifetime, white public opinion went from supporting segregation to recognizing integration as a positive good. Ask most white people in the housing market, and they will say they want to live in racially integrated communities. But they don't. Somewhere in between their stated desires and their actions is where the story of white racial hierarchy slips in—sometimes couched in the neutral-sounding terms of "good schools" or "appealing neighborhoods" or other codes for a racialized preference for homogeneity—and turns them back from their vision of an integrated life, with all its attendant benefits. It's a story that the law wrote in the mind and on the land through generations of mandated segregation.

THE BENEFITS OF INTEGRATION

But what if the entire logic is wrong? What if white people are not only paying too high a cost for segregation, but they're also mistaken about the benefit? Here's where things get interesting. Compared to students at predominantly white schools, white students who attend diverse K–12 schools achieve better learning outcomes and even higher test scores, particularly in areas such as math and science. Why? Of course, white students at racially diverse schools develop more cultural competency—the ability to collaborate and feel at ease with people from different racial, ethnic, and economic backgrounds—than students who attend segregated schools. But their minds are also improved when it comes to critical thinking and problem solving. Exposure to multiple viewpoints leads to more flexible and creative thinking and greater ability to solve problems.

The dividends of diversity in education pay out over a lifetime. Cultural competency is a necessity in today's multicultural professional world. In the long run, research reveals that racially diverse K–12 schools can produce better citizens—white students who feel a greater sense of civic engagement, who are more likely to consider friends and colleagues from different races as part of "us" rather than "them," who will be more at ease in the multicolor future of America in which white people will no longer be the majority. The benefits of diversity are not zero-sum gains for white people at the expense of their classmates of color, either. Amherst College psychology professor Dr. Deborah Son Holoien cites several studies of college students—the largest of which included more than seventy-seven thousand undergraduates—in which racially and ethnically diverse educational experiences resulted in improvements in critical thinking and learning outcomes, and in the acquisition of intellectual, scientific, and professional skills. The results were similar for black, white, Asian American, and Latinx students.

THE SOLIDARITY DIVIDEND IN SCHOOLS

My journey introduced me to families who are discovering the Solidarity Dividend in integrated schools. Because the dominant narrative about school quality is color-blind—the conversation is about numerical test scores and teacher-student ratios, not race or culture, of course—it's easy to walk right into a trap set for us by racism. It's an easy walk for millions of white parents who don't consider themselves racist. It was even an easy walk for Ali Takata, a mother of two who doesn't even consider herself white.

"Full disclosure I'm fifty percent white," she wrote in an introductory email. "I'm Hapa—Japanese and Italian. My husband is Sri Lankan, born in Singapore and raised in Singapore and England. Even though we are a mixed Asian family," she freely acknowledged,

"I've approached public school as a privileged [half-white] person. Depending on the situation, I am white-passing, although it's always hard to know how people perceive me."

Ali and her family moved from the San Francisco Bay Area to Austin, Texas, so her husband could begin a new job at the University of Texas. Ali researched the area, using school-rating resources such as GreatSchools.org to find what she then considered "a good neighborhood and a good school" for their two daughters, who were in preschool and first grade, respectively.

"Austin is divided east and west," Ali said. "And the farther west you go, the wealthier and the whiter the city becomes. The farther east you go, the more impoverished and browner and blacker the people are." This was no accident, she explained. "The 1928 Austin city plan segregated the city, forcing the black residents east. Then Interstate Thirty-five was built as a barrier to subjugate the black and brown residents even further. So . . . historically I-35 was the divide between east and west."

Ali's family could have paid less for a home in East Austin, where the school ratings were lower, but instead, they found a house in what she described as "a white, wealthy neighborhood" on the west side of Austin. Ali herself had grown up in a similar community, in a suburb of Hartford, Connecticut. As someone who is part white and part Asian, she had never felt totally comfortable there. But everything was nudging her to choose a similar world for her kids: the social conditioning, the data, even the signals that our market-based society sends about higher-priced things simply being better.

So, the Austin neighborhood Ali chose in order to find a "good" school ended up being very much like suburban Connecticut in the 1980s. "I recall specifically feeling like something was wrong with my eyes," said Ali. "Where were the Asian people? And where were the black people? They were virtually invisible here. . . . And it was just because I live on the west side."

She sent her kids to the local public school, whose student body reflected the neighborhood. "I will say that the first year was great," Ali said. "I found the people very welcoming. . . . It took me about a year to find a niche at that school, among the white wealthy people. But I did, you know. And I called them friends."

And yet, certain aspects of the school's culture began to disturb her. Parents were deeply involved in the school—not only fundraising and volunteering, but intruding into the school day in ways that seemed to Ali like "helicopter parenting." Parents tried to "micromanage the teachers and curriculum," Ali saw, to "insert themselves into the inner workings of the school, and to assume that 'I know just as much or more than the teacher or administrator.'"

It slowly dawned on her that many of the behaviors of both students and parents that she found off-putting were expressions of white privilege. "I feel like there's a way in which we upper-middle-class parents . . . want [our kids] to be unencumbered in their lives," including, she feels, by rules. "It's this entitlement. And it's this feeling of . . . is there a rule? I don't need to respect this rule. It doesn't pertain to me."

By her children's third year in the school, Ali realized, "'I just can't do this. This is not me.' It just—I felt kind of disgusted by the culture." It was everywhere, and yet she didn't have a name for it until she became involved in an affinity group for parents choosing integrated schools. "The competitiveness, complete with humble bragging. The insularity and superficiality, the focus on 'me and my kid only,'" Ali said. "By staying at [that] school, I was supporting a white-supremacy institution. That felt so wrong." Yet virtually her entire social circle in Austin was composed of parents who were active in the school and immersed in its values.

She began to research alternatives, visiting eight public schools on Austin's East Side, where her daughters would not be "surrounded by all that privilege," Ali said. "I was going to make this decision to desegregate my kids. You know, if the city wasn't going to do it, there's no policy around it, then I was going to do it.

"It was a very lonely process. I didn't talk to anybody about it except for my husband." The next fall, Ali and her husband transferred their daughters, then in second and fourth grade, to a school that was 50 percent African American, 30 percent Latinx, 11 percent white, 3 percent Asian, and 5 percent students of two or more races. Eighty-seven percent of the students were economically disadvantaged.

Ali's daughters are mixed Asian, with features and skin tones that make it unlikely they will be perceived by others as white, the way Ali sometimes is. At their old school or the new one, she said, "My girls will always go to school with kids who look different from them." Still, "I did not want to raise my girls in such a homogenous, unrealistic community. . . . I wanted them to experience difference."

The new school, she said, is predominantly "Black and brown, and that is what . . . permeates the school. There's music playing right when you walk in. Fun music, hip-hop music. And there's a step team." Ali values that her children will not grow up ignorant of the culture of their peers on the other side of town, but the advantages of the new school go much deeper than music and dance. "It's also more community-focused, which is antithetical to the white, privileged culture" of making sure my child gets the best of everything.

As for the parents in the West Austin neighborhood, "there has been a deafening silence around my decision." When she runs into some of her former friends, they may talk about how their children are doing, but they don't ask her anything at all about hers. "The white community I left felt stifling and oppressive," Ali said. "That part surprised me. My profound relief surprised me. I had no idea that living my values would feel so liberating."

Transferring to a new school in which they are surrounded by kids with different experiences and frames of reference has had its bumps, but it "has been an eye-opening experience for [my girls], I think," Ali said. "And it has brought up really healthy [family] discussions . . . about wealth and class and how it feels for them . . . to be called [out] for being the rich kids. . . . I think it's been an amazing experience."

Integrated Schools is a nationwide grassroots effort to empower, educate, and organize parents who are white and/or privileged like Ali, parents who want to shift their priorities about their children's education away from centering metrics like test scores or assumptions about behavior and discipline and toward contributing to an antiracist public educational system. The movement acknowledges that "white parents have been the key barrier to the advancement of school integration and education equity." Through resources including reading lists and guides for awkward conversations, along with traditional community organizing and coalition-building tactics, the movement encourages parents not to view "diversity primarily as a commodity for the benefit of our own children" and not to view schools that serve primarily students of color as "broken and in need of white parents to fix them." Rather, the goal of leveraging parents' choices about schools should be to disrupt segregation because of the ways it distorts our democracy and corrodes the prospects of all our children. The group offers tools and tips to enable parents to live their values and to raise antiracist children who can help build an antiracist future.

As for Ali Takata, she lost a circle of friends but gained something far more valuable. "Through my experience at the new school, I've been able to see how steeped in white upper-middle-class culture I had been," she said. And now, "Oh my goodness, I cannot believe the peace I feel with my decision and my life."

THIS IS HOW IT'S SUPPOSED TO BE

Sending her two children to the local public schools twenty-something years ago wasn't so much a decision for Tracy Wright-Mauer, a white woman who moved to Poughkeepsie, New York, when her husband got a job at IBM. It was more of a decision not to act, not to pull her children away from the urban neighborhood she fell in love with, with its beautiful old homes. "My husband and I, we didn't consciously say, 'Okay. We're going to . . . be, you know, be the integrators,' or anything. We just didn't think not to buy a house in the district, and we didn't think, 'Oh, well, I'll send my kids to private school [because] the school doesn't look like my kids.'" The most thought she ever gave to it was when other white parents would ask her questions such as "Well, when you get to middle school, are you going to send them to private school?" or "What about high school? You're going to send them to Lourdes, right?"—referring to the nearly 90 percent white Catholic school.

Many of these white parents had purchased their houses in Spackenkill, a wealthy part of Poughkeepsie that fought for school district independence in the 1960s and '70s. Spackenkill successfully sued to keep its district separate from the larger city, walling off its richer tax base (including the revenues from the IBM headquarters). One can find similar stories all across the country, with predominantly white school districts drawing narrower boundaries to serve far fewer children (typically just fifteen hundred) than majority of-color low-income districts that serve an average of over ten thousand. It's a hoarding of resources by white families who wouldn't have such a wealth advantage if it weren't for generations of explicit racial exclusion and predation in the housing market.

A few years ago, Tracy was cleaning her house and came across her daughter's second-grade class photo: fifteen smiling prepubescent boys and girls in their Photo Day best. She snapped a picture and posted it on Facebook, and one of her black friends pointed out to her that "other than the teachers, [Fiona] was the only white kid in the class." Her daughter, Fiona, is now in college; her son, Aidan, is wrapping up high school. They're both the products of what parents in the Integrated Schools Facebook group Tracy now belongs to call Global Majority public schools, and "both have learned to discuss race," she offered. "They talk about it all the time. They discuss class. They discuss racism and equity, and they just are really, really engaged with their friends about these subjects. And, you know, I think it's pretty awesome."

I had to ask Tracy the million-dollar question: Were they good schools? What about the standardized test scores, the yardstick by which all quality is measured? Tracy didn't pause: "Maybe I'm an anomaly. I think other parents look to the test scores . . . to judge a school. Just because the test scores are not, you know, the highest in the state, or in the top ten, it doesn't mean to me that the kids aren't getting really great teachers and being challenged and doing interesting things in their classes." Her son, Aidan, who was graduating the year we spoke, is the only white guy in his friend group, and all his friends were going on to college. "His friends are smart kids who work hard, and they do well on their SATs, and they're very motivated."

I was able to reach Fiona, a freshman on a rowing scholarship at Drexel University in Philadelphia, in her dorm room. I asked her what it had been like going to a high school where just 10 percent of the student body was white. Fiona recalled it making for some uncomfortable conversations with white kids in other school districts. They'd go something like this: "I'd say, oh, I'm from Poughkeepsie

[High],' and they'd be like, 'Oh, I'm so sorry.' Which someone actually said to me." I cringed. "It's really just disappointing. Because I love Poughkeepsie [High], and I loved my time there, and the friends I made."

Fiona said her direction in life had been influenced by how she learned to see the world at Poughkeepsie High; she credited the experience with giving her the skills to be an advocate. "It helped me empathetically. I don't know if I want to be a politician, or if I want to work with some environmental justice organization, but empathy has a lot to do with that: looking at both sides of the story and not trying to put a Band-Aid over something, but getting to the root of the problem. I think that's where my skills lie. And . . . a lot of that comes from where I grew up and where I went to school."

Fiona's now at a college where more than half of the students are white, and just 8 and 6 percent are African American and Latinx, respectively. It's a big shift. Many of her white peers are just not as comfortable around people of color. "If there's a roomful of black people and [we walk in and] we're the only white people? I think they sort of say—like, 'Oh, like, let's leave.' Or they say, like, if we're out at night, 'Oh, this is, like, a little sketchy.' Things like that, I notice." But she also doesn't want to suggest that white kids who grew up in segregated schools are hopeless when it comes to race. "I think one of the downfalls of growing up in a homogeneous setting is that the process of understanding . . . racial inequalities and recognizing one's own privilege can be very uncomfortable and might take longer, but it doesn't mean they don't get there."

In that way, Fiona feels lucky. "I got to spend my time with people who didn't look like me, and that didn't really matter. And I hope to strive to feel that way throughout my whole life. To not be surprised when I'm in a diverse group of people, and just be like, 'This is normal. This is how it's supposed to be.'"

CHAPTER 8

THE SAME SKY

I USED TO THINK THAT THE UNITED STATES WAS SUPERMAN, the hero who would always rise to save the world when it was threatened. But today, climate change is like a meteor hurtling toward planet Earth and the US is refusing to leap to the rescue. How did our country lose our superhero status in the fight of our lives? We are the biggest carbon polluter in history, but we have one of the most politically powerful factions opposed to taking action to prevent catastrophic climate change. In our peer countries, the conservative political parties draw contrast with the center and left by advocating for corporate climate solutions over government programs and regulations. Only in the United States does our conservative party, with very few exceptions, flat-out deny that there's a problem. The opposition of the American conservative political movement is the primary reason the United States has not taken stronger legislative action to reduce greenhouse gases; our inaction is one of the main reasons the world has continued to warm.

In short, the loss of human and animal life and habitats that we are already experiencing is in no small part due to the American conservative political faction. And that political faction is almost entirely white.

Yet there's more to the story. I asked my friend May Boeve, a cofounder of one of the newer big climate groups, 350.org, whether she saw climate change denial as an identity issue. "Honestly, I don't know that anybody in the Big Greens [the nickname for the biggest national environmental organizations] does. We see that it's become a partisan issue, for sure—and we are very aware that communities of color are being hit first and worst by climate impacts. But generally speaking, our field sees race impacting climate as a disparities issue, not a racial politics issue."

May's organization was cofounded by a white climate expert named Bill McKibben and a group of white Middlebury College students from Vermont in 2009, with the aim of mobilizing hundreds of countries into mass action for climate solutions. It operates in 180 countries, training mostly young people for demonstrations that have included anti–Keystone Pipeline rallies, the People's Climate March in 2014, and the global climate strike in 2019. The global, multicultural scope of 350.org's work, combined with its years of partnership with Indigenous climate activists, has spurred its leadership to deepen their racial justice analysis. So, as I set out to determine what was going on with the connection between racism and opposition to climate action, I promised to share with May what I was learning.

It turns out that white people in America are much less likely than people of color to rank environmental problems as a pressing concern. Public opinion surveys show that black and Latinx people are more supportive of national and international climate change solutions than white people are. In fact, if it were up to only white people, we might not act at all. According to the Yale Project on Climate Change Communication, fewer than 25 percent of white people said they were willing to join a campaign to convince government to act on climate change. The majority of white Americans fell into the categories the researchers called "Cautious," "Disengaged," "Doubtful," or "Dismissive," meaning they don't know enough, don't care, or are outright opposed to taking action. By contrast, 70 percent of Latinx and 57 percent of black people are either "Alarmed" or "Concerned." Like so many issues in public life, race appears to significantly shape your worldview about climate change.

When I shared this and other research about race and climate viewpoints with May Boeve on a phone call, she was reflective. "Maybe it's because, despite the prominence of so many leaders of color, white environmentalists play such an outsize role in the Big Green leadership. This"—how resistant white Americans are to taking action—"remains a blind spot for the mainstream environmental movement," she told me.

"In some ways, it makes sense," I replied. "The same power structures that advantage white people in the world are advantaging white people in the advocacy field, and the cost of that is that the field is not seeing where the biggest untapped base is for organizing."

"It's interesting," May said, "because 350 is a global organization, so I do spend a lot of time thinking about how culture shapes different people's worldviews and what will move them to action. . . . It's different in Bangladesh versus Hong Kong versus Egypt versus the US, or the many communities within each of those places. But, of course, the most powerful worldview we need to contend with is white supremacy. Of course it is," she said, then added with a little laugh, "and the patriarchy." Indeed, the Yale Project on Climate Change Communication found that of the six categories of American opinion about climate change, the "Dismissive" were more likely to be white, male, and have higher incomes.

But why? My first instinct is always to follow the money and power: Are powerful interests using race to sell climate denialism to white people?

In an influential 2011 study cheekily named "Cool Dudes," the researchers Aaron M. McCright and Riley E. Dunlap examined public opinion data from the period of 2000 to 2010 and found that conservative white men were much more likely to be climate change deniers. The researchers attributed it not to any biological difference, of course, but rather, to the story that white men receive from elite white males in the political media with whom they identify, and the story they tend to believe about themselves, which they described as "identity-protection cognition" and a "system-justification" worldview that is resistant to change. McCright and Dunlap wrote, "Conservative white males are likely to favor protection of the current industrial capitalist order which has historically served them well."

I thought about the many, many moments in my career when politically moderate or conservative white men, whether in Congress or in the editorial pages, had weighed in against action on some social good—environmental protection, raising revenue for public investment, consumer financial regulation—by claiming that it would be "bad for the economy." Our side always had to then jump through hoops to make elaborate statistical models proving that it wouldn't be costly or that it would create jobs and stimulate overall economic growth. But what dawned on me, when I read the research showing that conservative white men tended to justify a system that had served them well, was that "the economy" they were referring to was *their* economy, the economic condition of people like them, seen through the lens of a zero-sum system of hierarchy that taught them to fear any hint of redistribution. Value-neutral admonitions about protecting "the economy" allowed them to protect their own status while resting easy knowing that they were not at all racist, because it wasn't about race—it was about, well, "the economy."

Perhaps it makes sense, if you've spent a lifetime seeing yourself as the winner of a zero-sum competition for status, that you would have learned along the way to accept inequality as normal; that you'd come to attribute society's wins and losses solely to the players' skill and merit. You might also learn that if there are problems, you and yours are likely to be spared the costs. The thing is, that's just not the case with the environment and climate change. We live under the same sky. Scorching triple-digit days, devastating wildfires, and drought restrictions on drinking water have become the new normal for California's working-class barrios and gated communities alike. Wall Street was flooded by Superstorm Sandy; most of the 13 million people with imperiled seafront housing on the coasts belong to the upper classes. The cash crops at the base of the American agribusiness economy are threatened by more frequent droughts. The majority of white Americans are skeptical or opposed to tackling climate change, but the majority of white Americans will suffer nonetheless from an increasingly inhospitable planet.

SACRIFICE ZONES

To accept that we live under the same sky is to reject the dominant US approach to environmental risk, which has been to shunt off the pollution by-products of industry to what are known as sacrifice zones. For nearly fifty years, grassroots activists living in these sacrifice zones—Richmond, California; Ocala, Florida; South Bronx, New York; Youngstown, Ohio, and many more—have been proving how racism shapes environmental policy. Collecting soil samples and keeping diaries of hospital visits, mapping the distance between incinerators and neighborhoods of color, they have built a damning record of environmental racism—and a movement for environmental justice.

I decided to travel to the San Francisco Bay Area city of Richmond, California, where a thriving cross-racial environmental justice movement has been taking on the city's rampant industrial pollution. Richmond is a sacrifice zone in the shadow of one of the country's largest oil refineries, with thirteen times as many air quality violations as the Bay Area's average over a decade. Miya Yoshitani, head of the Asian Pacific Environmental Network (APEN), reminded me that any story about sacrifice zones must start with an explanation of the decisions that created clusters of people of color to target in the first place. "These places are government creations to begin with, that are created by racist policy. . . . And people always want to say, 'People of color, they're poor, and so therefore they live in the less desirable places.' Well, you know . . . those less desirable places were the only places that they could legally own homes. . . . They're not accidental. . . . Those are intentional."

As Richard Rothstein documents in his book *The Color of Law*, Richmond is one of the quintessential stories of government-created American segregation. It was an epicenter of American manufacturing during World War II, and so the government quickly created twenty-four thousand units of low-rent public housing—some exclusively for white workers and some for everybody else. Once the rental units reached capacity, the government contracted with a private developer to create a nearby suburban development, called Rollingwood, of higher-quality, permanent housing that white workers could lease or purchase. The Federal Housing Authority guaranteed the developer's financing on the condition that none of the seven hundred new homes be sold to anyone "not wholly of the Caucasian race." Barred by law from living in most of the rapidly developing county, black workers and their families were forced into an area known as North Richmond. North Richmond was an unincorporated area—meaning, not an official town at all, with no government services whatsoever: no roads, streetlights, water, or sewage. The African American wartime workers had to fend entirely for themselves while their white coworkers had all their housing needs met by government subsidy, policy, and planning.

The lines of opportunity and place that a racist government policy drew in the mid-1940s remain in Richmond to this day. In a county rimmed with suburbs that excluded black families, the city became predominantly black during the war. The manufacturing and chemical processing plants that created jobs and opportunity in the war era have either closed or become far less labor-intensive, so that Richmond is left with the worst of both worlds: few middle-class jobs and lots of toxic pollution, including abandoned waste. Richmond residents "live within a ring of five major oil re-fineries, three chemical companies, eight Superfund sites, dozens of other toxic waste sites, highways, two rail yards, ports and marine terminals where tankers dock"—some 350 toxic sites in all. The polluter that's most synonymous with Richmond, however, is the one-hundred-plus-year-old Chevron refinery, also the dominant player in Richmond politics.

Today, North Richmond is 97 percent black, Latinx, or Asian and, amazingly, still unincorporated. Displacement and poverty have often created tensions across these communities, but activists have helped their neighbors see a common threat to unite them: the polluters in everyone's backyard. Since forging a multiracial coalition to take control of their city council and take on Chevron, Richmond community groups have won for their residents probably the most important Solidarity Dividend there is: the chance for better health.

To learn more about Richmond, Miya suggested I go for a drive with Torm Nompraseurt, the longest-serving staff member of APEN and one of the first Laotian refugees to the United States. (He arrived in 1975.) I met Torm on a Sunday afternoon at the local museum, where an exhibit about Richmond's Laotian community was opening. Wearing a black traditional Laotian suit with red trim, Torm greeted me in Lao-accented English, all soft consonants riding on a melodic cadence. He generously introduced me to other community activists of every racial and ethnic background, and he had a hard time making his exit from a gathering where everybody seemed to know his name.

Torm finally said his last goodbyes and led me into his well-used red car for a drive around his neighborhood on the "fence line" abutting the massive Chevron refinery. As we drove, I saw few people out: the day was bright but windy and cold, and besides, from what I could see, there was little to attract them on the street. A chronically disinvested city, Richmond has no full-service grocery store within walking distance. I don't recall even seeing a corner deli during our nearly hour-long drive around the fence-line neighborhood. What you see most, however, is industry: salvage lots, tankers, freight cars, a massive garbage dump, and factories . . . so many factories, making pesticides and other chemicals, with none bigger than the nearly three-thousand-acre sprawling complex where Chevron refines about 250,000 barrels of crude oil a day.

We pulled up near an elementary school. In 1996, Richmond's African American community (spearheaded by Henry Clark, the veteran organizer of the West County Toxics Coalition) won a long battle to close a Chevron incinerator just behind the schoolyard. Even though Chevron has gotten rid of the unnerving sight of incinerator smokestacks jutting up behind a playground structure, the school is still just about a mile from the refinery. Its nearest neighbors are an oil distributor and a chemicals testing lab. Richmond children are hospitalized for asthma at almost twice the rate of those in neighboring areas. (The school is one of the worst-performing in the state, and research increasingly demonstrates a significant link between air quality and student performance.)

Richmond has disproportionately high rates of heart disease and cancer; the plant's closest neighbors are in the ninety-ninth percentile for asthma rates. The city has the double whammy of fixed and mobile pollution—it not only has an inordinate number of toxic industrial sites, but it's surrounded on all sides by highways. I asked Torm about his own health. "I am coughing all the time. You know, the Laotians, especially the young kids or the elders, have a lot of asthma and coughing and respiratory issues and so on and so forth. . . . [I]n the Laotian community, we have a member, someone who just passed this morning because she had cancer. . . . Most of the time when our members die, often eighty percent, ninety percent, the doctors say, 'Well, because of cancer.'"

Torm turned his car onto one of the freeways so that he could drive the length of the Chevron facility, which is awe-inspiring in its breadth and glittering detail. The fence surrounding Chevron is six miles long. The plant complex looks like a science-fiction city unto itself, with structures of every different shape interlaced with pipes and tubes, all accented with flickering lights and plumes of smoke. Thirty-odd massive round holding tanks dot the hillside behind it, each painted a burnt umber in a beautification effort to blend them into the surroundings. (That paint job is an unfortunately apt metaphor for corporate social responsibility efforts that are only cosmetic; the darker color wound up making the tanks absorb more heat, leading to *more* toxic evaporation.) The Chevron plant spews over a thousand pounds of chemicals into the air on a good day. Then there are the bad days.

"On August sixth, 2012, when the siren came on . . . ," Torm told me, "I know that's not testing, because [they test on] Wednesday. And so, I know right away in my heart . . . this is real. And of course, I closed my door and the window and everything and do the shelter-in-place protocol. You put a towel on [the] bottom of the door, to make sure that the air doesn't come in your house, and close all the doors and windows.

"It's about a quarter mile from Chevron to my apartment at that time. And then I saw a couple [of] people who ran outside. They were Laotian, who live in the same apartment complex. They ran outside and kind of looked at the smoke. And I opened the door and yelled at them and said, 'You cannot go out. Get in your house, and close the door and window and put a towel in your door right away, right now!' And then they said, 'What?' I said, 'It's a Chevron fire. It's chemical. Go in your house!'"

The 2012 Chevron fire was caused by a leak from a degraded pipe that Chevron knew for years was at risk of corrosion. Internal recommendations to inspect and replace the pipes because of a common type of sulfur degradation went unheeded for nearly a decade. What began as a drip in the afternoon ended with a fire that sent plumes of chemical smoke into the community's air, in clouds visible for miles. The chemicals that Chevron cast to the wind that day reached not just Torm and his neighbors in the fence-line community, nearest to the refinery, but also three neighboring towns. Medical providers and hospitals reported seeing fifteen thousand people sickened by the fumes in the coming days.

Torm exited the freeway and turned up a steep hill to get a better view of the refinery. As his old car revved up the slope, it seemed the house values were climbing as well. "These houses seem like they're more expensive, maybe," I ventured as we passed a pink house with a Mercedes in the driveway.

"Yes. This is called Point Richmond. [This is] the rich community in Richmond."

GOOD FOR WHITE FOLKS, TOO

Point Richmond is on the southwest edge of the city, a neighborhood up a hill that slopes down into a nature preserve along the harbor. With the median price of houses at $816,000 in 2020, the area is a segregated cluster of mostly white homeowners. Sitting in Torm's car, however, looking at the way the refinery towers could be seen over the million-dollar rooflines, I couldn't help but wonder: Aren't these white people breathing the same air? I asked him about it.

"Well, you know, it's a very interesting question you ask. Because the wind pattern—it always blows toward North Richmond," the unincorporated area that's almost all people of color. "And so, the people who live in Point Richmond—somehow they feel like the wind is doing them a favor, never flows down to their community," Torm said, and I chuckled at the image of a wind with favors to give.

"[But] one of the years that . . . a Chevron accident happened . . . somehow the wind happened to blow down to their side. And I remember, oh my God, they're screaming and yelling. And then we told them, 'See? Now you know what we mean.'"

Richmond has three community air quality monitors around the city, each one in a neighborhood occupying one rung of the city's stratification. One is in wealthy Point Richmond, another in the still-unincorporated area of North Richmond, and the third in Atchison Village, an affordable housing complex built during the war exclusively for white workers that's now a cooperative, home to mostly white seniors and Latinx families. I dug into the data, expecting to see that Point Richmond was largely spared the toxicity that permeated the other areas of the city, but that wasn't the case. In terms of the number of toxins recorded in the air and the number of days with toxins present, there wasn't much difference between the three neighborhoods. While the saturation levels may have varied as the wind blew—the data didn't show—the white part of Richmond was indeed still living under the same sky.

A 2012 study showed that this dynamic was borne out nationwide. Called "Is Environmental Justice Good for White Folks? Industrial Air Toxics and Exposure in Urban America," the study compared pollution levels by neighborhood in cities and found that the sacrifice zones had more spillover than one might expect. I reached out to one of the study's authors, Professor Michael Ash at the University of Massachusetts, to talk about what the researchers had discovered. "We wanted in particular to focus on places that had very unequal exposure," he explained to me. In places where it was "easier, for reasons of the power structure, to displace environmental bads onto vulnerable communities, [we wanted to know] are those [the] places that tend to rack up a higher environmental bill across the board?"

He went on: "Not shockingly, places that are unequal are much worse for the socially vulnerable party, but they also turn out to be worse for at least some members of the socially less vulnerable classes."

Environmental racism, in other words, was bad for better-off white people, too. I asked Professor Ash how it worked. While the study proved correlation, not causation, he believed it was a question of power. He described the elite mindset: "Don't worry, this pollution can be displaced onto the Other, onto the wrong side of the environmental tracks. So . . . put on blinders, don't pay too much attention to the gross amount of pollution that is being produced."

It made sense. If a set of decision-makers believes that an environmental burden can be shouldered by someone else to whom they don't feel connected or accountable, they won't think it's worthwhile to minimize the burden by, for example, forcing industry to put controls on pollution. But that results in a system that creates more pollution than would exist if decision-makers cared about everyone equally—and we're talking about air, water, and soil, where it's pretty hard to cordon off toxins completely to the so-called sacrifice zone. It's elites' blindness to the costs they pay that keeps pollution higher for everyone. Professor Ash let exasperation creep into his voice when he said, "We have the idea that this environmental bad can be displaced onto a socially excluded community, that primes the pump for doing more of it. And then you end up with uncontrollable amounts that are bad absolutely for everyone."

What's most frustrating to Professor Ash is that the other side of the ledger—the cost of preventing pollution and saving lives—is usually so small. "The non–trade-offs are what is shocking here. I mean, we are just—for chump change, we are exposing people to these terrible toxins. . . . It just wouldn't be that expensive to give everybody a clean and healthy environment."

THE ENVIRONMENTAL SOLIDARITY DIVIDEND

In the early 2000s, Richmond activists representing different causes and ethnic communities joined together to make a plan to take on Chevron—but they had a lot of mistrust and division to overcome.

Chevron had polluted the politics of the city, both by controlling the city council and by cultivating relationships with local groups in ways that activists called cynical and racially divisive. Torm and Miya said that Chevron lobbyists had learned how to pit community groups against each other for small funding grants and scholarships, which Torm likened to Chevron's "throw[ing] candy on the floor to get a kid fighting."

Through hard work and relationship-building, the Richmond Progressive Alliance was born. "And that's when we launched a . . . strategy to recruit and support a [city council] candidate who would not take corporate money,"Torm told me with triumph in his voice. "Chevron was dominant because they used a lot of money to buy the community leaders to work for their candidates. But then we launched the campaign to tell people that unless we change the city council decision-making, we cannot fight. We can be screaming and yelling [in community meetings] until four in the morning, and the city council still votes the way Chevron wants them to."

The coalition proposed and vetted candidates, endorsed, knocked on doors, and convinced some of the most overlooked neighborhoods in Richmond to turn out for a progressive slate for the city council. "We were able to kick out the 'Chevron Five' and get a progressive majority into city council," Miya recalls. The coalition's most remarkable achievement was the election of Green Party mayor Gayle McLaughlin, a white woman, who became a thorn in Chevron's side. Permits and programs that for decades had sailed through approval suddenly met with more inquiry, investigations, hearings, and even lawsuits. When the company sought to create a

$1-billion-plus plant expansion for processing the heavier, higher-sulfur crude oil that gas companies increasingly rely on, the coalition sued and won because Chevron hadn't provided enough information about the pollution impact. "It put the refinery into a major panic," recalled Miya. The pressure forced an environmental impact assessment and changes to the plan that would reduce emissions and guarantee certain benefits to the community.

Torm drove me past a stunning sixty-acre field of solar panels outside the refinery gates. Called MCE Solar One, it's part of the community benefits agreement the coalition won and one of the more visible signs of the new day in Richmond. The public owns and generates the low-cost solar energy for residents, which lowers their utility bills and pollution. The solar array was built with 50 percent local labor in partnership with a training program that prepared hundreds of Richmond residents for clean-energy jobs.

"It's not just one solar project," Miya told me. "These local models of Just Transition have started to really grow." Just Transition is a concept first formulated by unions to protect jobs in industries facing environmental regulations in the late 1990s, but environmental justice advocates have adopted it as a way to express the idea that the shift away from a fossil fuel economy doesn't have to mean massive job losses. In fact, a Just Transition must create good jobs and build community wealth for the low-income communities and people of color who have disproportionately suffered under the current polluting economy.

When Miya described the progress in Richmond and the community's vision for remaking their economy, it seemed like such a win-win to me. Save the planet, create new jobs, build community wealth—what's not to love? But that's not how the climate change opposition sees it. For them, it is a zero-sum competition between the environment and the economy as it is. Or perhaps, as the sociologists argue, it's deeper than that: a zero sum between the winners of the hierarchy today and those who are just fighting for air.

The good news is that the type of multiracial coalition that has begun to loosen Chevron's grip on Richmond is starting to assemble across the nation, putting within sight a Solidarity Dividend for people and the planet. Momentum has been growing at the grass roots. A historic assembly of people from an array of Indigenous communities, putting aside tribal differences and led by Native youth, camped at Standing Rock to protest the Dakota Access Pipeline and build power for Indigenous-led environmental protection. Environmental justice groups led by people of color forced conversations with the Big Greens and their funders about who gets the resources and sets the strategy for the movement. Young people staged record-breaking strikes and protests for climate action across the world. The leaders who are the most committed to saving the planet finally got together to hash out their differences and discover places of mutual interest: labor unions and conservationists, Big Greens and grassroots environmental justice groups, and Native-led groups and youth activists.

Siloed and often at cross purposes, these groups weren't powerful enough to take on the strategic deployment of white identity politics backed by fossil fuel billions, but now they're linking arms around a shared vision of a sustainable, just transition from fossil fuels that guarantees economic security for all those who are suffering—whether they're asthmatic schoolkids of color or, yes, coal miners. That vision is popular with 59 percent of the population. Multiracial coalitions in cities and states have won versions of the Green New Deal, which focuses on public policy to address climate change, along with other social aims like reducing economic inequality, in California, New Mexico, New York, and Washington.

May Boeve came to visit me at home in the fall of 2019, bringing a beautiful knit blanket for my newborn son—and for me: good news about how the climate movement was changing from the inside. As we sat on my couch drinking tea, I felt that she was as optimistic as I'd ever seen her. "It was naive, looking back on it now," May said with her brow furrowed, "but we didn't realize how much racism was holding us back from building the kind of coalition we needed to win. We're trying to make sure that the whole field never makes that mistake again."

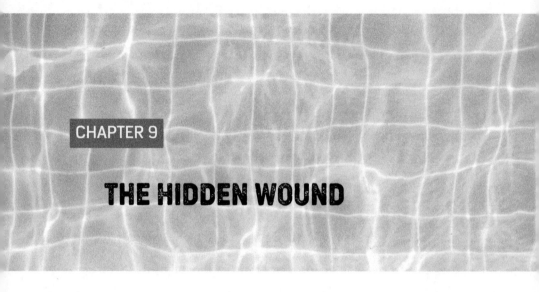

CHAPTER 9

THE HIDDEN WOUND

HAVE AN INDELIBLE MEMORY FROM MIDDLE SCHOOL. WE were in the auditorium, watching the PBS documentary about the civil rights struggle, *Eyes on the Prize*. The grainy black-and-white images showed a veritable pantheon onscreen: Rosa Parks, the Rev. Dr. Martin Luther King Jr., and the unnamed heroes withstanding abuse at a lunch counter or leaning up against a wall, shielding their faces from the spray from water hoses. Every February, for Black History Month, our school put on a display of the righteousness of black Americans. The organ struck up, and the white students looked to the lyrics in their programs. When we finished singing "Lift Ev'ry Voice and Sing," the black national anthem, Vanessa, a white girl in my sixth-grade class, turned to me and whispered, "I wish I was black."

To an eleven-year-old, this must have seemed like the inevitable conclusion to the morality play we'd just seen. Who would want to be one of the bad guys? Compared to freckle-faced Vanessa, my darker skin would afford me little privilege in life, except in one arena: the privilege of being born among the heroes in the American story of social progress, not among the villains. I never had to watch documentary footage of people who looked like my parents, their faces contorted in fury, hurling abuse at a little girl going to school. But Vanessa had—and the clear moral contrast made her want to switch sides. What's often forgotten, however, is that the bad guys on-screen believed that they were doing what was morally right.

It's just human nature: we all like to see ourselves as on the side of the heroes in a story. But for white Americans today who are awake to the reality of American racism, that's nearly impossible. That's a moral cost of racism that millions of white people bear and that those of us who've borne every other cost of racism simply don't. It can cause contradictions and justifications, feelings of guilt, shame, projection, resentment, and denial. Ultimately, though, we are all paying for the moral conflict of white Americans.

Over the years that I have sought answers to why a fairer economy is so elusive, it has become clearer to me that how white people understand what's right and wrong about our diverse nation, who belongs and who deserves, is determining our collective course. This is the crux of it: Can we swim together in the same pool or not? It's a political question, yes, and one with economic ramifications. But at its core, it's a moral question. Ultimately, an economy—the rules we abide by and set for what's fair and who merits what—is an expression of our moral understanding. So, if our country's moral compass is broken, is it any wonder that our economy is adrift?

Angela King grew up in a rural all-white area of South Florida. She had learned pretty much every form of prejudice from her parents—"homophobia, racism, stereotypes, racial slurs," she told me. "I grew up thinking that was normal. And I grew up with an abnormal fear of people who weren't like me." I wondered about how she went from being afraid of people her parents had taught her were foreign to organizing her life around hating and terrorizing them.

Angela told me that she was bullied in school, and when she was twelve, it turned physical. "The school bully ripped my shirt open in front of the entire class, and here I was," Angela recalled, "this pudgy little girl in her training bra. And it did something to me. It provoked this rage that I really didn't know I had inside. So, I fought that bully back, and unfortunately that day, I became the bully." She told herself, "If I'm the one doing those kind of things, no one can ever humiliate me like that again."

In high school, Angela sought a place to fit in. She eventually chose a group that displayed swastikas and Confederate flags. "And honestly, I wasn't attracted to them because of the beliefs," she said. But "they were the one group I found that never questioned my anger or my aggression or my violence. They just accepted it. I never had to explain it or account for it. And that began my life in the violent far right." She was fifteen years old.

When I asked her how she justified her actions, she explained that she simply accepted the opportunity that the story of white supremacy has always offered: a way to shift the blame. Regarding slavery, for instance, she said, "I found a way to blame [it] on those who were enslaved . . . [saying] things like 'Africans sold their own people, so they deserve to be enslaved.'"

Angela discovered that Nazism gave her not only a justification for the race-based hierarchy of human value she believed in, but also a ready scapegoat for every disappointment in her life. At age twenty-three, she wound up in a federal detention center, sentenced for taking part in an armed robbery targeting a Jewish store owner. "And I not only didn't feel responsible," she recalled, "but [I] was at a place where . . . nothing was my responsibility. It was my parents' fault. It was black people taking my good jobs, even though I was a high school dropout, a drunk."

But inside prison, her all-white world was gone. She recalls saying aloud, "Now I'm the minority." One day, Angela was smoking by herself in the recreation yard when a black woman looked over at her. Angela, who was covered in racist tattoos, thought, "Oh, she's gonna start something." But instead, the woman invited her to play cards.

"And from that point on, we started a friendship," Angela said. "We didn't really talk about why we were there for a long time . . . about the fact that I came in there as a skinhead for a hate crime. . . . Even knowing that, this group of women treated me as a human being. I had no idea how to react to that. I couldn't find justification in the usual aggression and violence that I used.

"They didn't let me slide for long, though. Eventually, the very hard conversations started to happen." The woman who had first befriended her "would just out of the blue ask me questions like, 'So, if you met me before we came to prison, and I was with my daughter, what would you have done to us? Would you have called me the N-word? Would you have tried to kill my daughter? Would you have tried to hurt me?' And being in prison, and with the friendship I [had] forged with some of them, I couldn't get up and run away and not answer the questions. So, I was forced into not only being honest with them, but . . . with myself."

When she was released from prison at age twenty-six, Angela put her former life behind her and threw herself into education. She ended up earning three degrees. "I learned a great bit about history and systemic racism and oppression and got a clear under-standing of the true history of our country. When I was growing up, I didn't get facts about how this country really began. I got the white version."

Angela became an activist, giving speeches around the country to share her story and cofounding an organization called Life After Hate, which helps people get out of violent white-supremacist groups. But the audience for her message is broader than neo-Nazis. She doesn't want the existence of violent, racist gangs to let white people in the political mainstream off the hook. "[We are all] socialized into a society where racism is normal, and it's built into every aspect of our democracy, our government, and our social systems. . . . There are so many white people that have no clue," she told me.

"And when . . . you try to give them a clue, they become very defensive. Because no one wants to think that they are benefiting from a system that hurts other people. It's much easier just to pre-tend like you don't know."

White supremacy had given Angela something she desperately needed in order to feel better about herself: scapegoats. I thought about the function that immigrants, particularly from Latin America, are playing in today's racial theater, being blamed for the loss of jobs and even the more diffuse "way of life." Fox News host Laura Ingraham told her audience of millions, "In some parts of the country, it does seem like the America that we know and love doesn't exist anymore," and blamed it on immigration. Tucker Carlson raged, "Our leaders demand that you shut up and accept this. We have a moral obligation to admit the world's poor, they tell us, even if it makes our own country poorer, and dirtier, and more divided."

Prominent white nationalists are clear that they want to maintain a white America, but most people justify having animus toward immigrants in a "nation of immigrants" in moral terms: it's not the immigrant part; it's the "illegal" part. They broke the law; they're criminals. As history shows us, once a group is criminalized, they're outside the circle of human concern. This moral story of law-abiding citizens and criminal immigrants hinges on people having, as Angela said, "no clue" about the racist structures that let the ancestors of many white Americans arrive with no restrictions or requirements save their whiteness, which extended to them ladders of opportunity upon arrival that were the exact opposite of the walls and shadows today's immigrant workers face. This story blames some of the least powerful people on the planet for a problem created and sustained by the most powerful—corporations profiting from sweatshop labor and policy-makers unwilling to update our immigration laws. Nonetheless, as it has for centuries, racism makes an immoral view of the world into a moral one. The elite adds in the urgency of the zero-sum story—they are taking what you have; they are a threat to you—and it's enough to keep a polity focused on scapegoats while no progress is made on the actual economic issues in most Americans' lives.

I thought about Melanie, a white woman I connected with on my journey via a mutual friend. Melanie is in her forties and grew up mostly in the rural Appalachian region of North Carolina amid her mother's large family, which she describes as "very conservative and very racist."

Melanie's family struggled financially and often lacked the money for heating oil or a telephone. "We knew the sick feeling of what a car breaking down felt like," she said. Melanie left her small town for college at age seventeen and never returned; her world, and her worldview, expanded. As an adult, she took it upon herself to help educate her mother out of the racist beliefs she had absorbed in her family and then cemented by listening to conservative talk radio.

"She used to tell me that it says in the Bible that there was a reason that black people were inferior," Melanie recalled. "And I basically got out the Bible and made her show me where it said that."

Melanie remembered a breakthrough moment when she was talking with her mother and stepfather. "They said something about 'the Mexicans,' and 'they all live in that house together,' you know, 'There are thirty-five people in that house.'

"And I sat down with them and had a conversation about what that looks like." They discussed the social and economic forces that might compel a large extended family, like their own, to live in one house. "And it's completely infuriating to me," Melanie said, "because we . . . didn't have any money. . . . We know economic pressures and the discrimination of being poor. And so, I just sort of laid it out for them like that, and they got it, you know? In a way that I don't think they had ever really thought about it before."

THE PROBLEM WITH COLORBLINDNESS

When Angela King was a skinhead, she saw race everywhere. But then again, so does everybody. The first thing you take in when you see someone is their skin color. Within a fraction of a second, that sight triggers your ingrained associations and prejudices. If those prejudices about a person's skin color are negative—as they overwhelmingly are among white people regarding darker skin—they alert your amygdala, the section of the brain responsible for anxiety and other emotions, to flood your body with adrenaline in a fight-or-flight response.

But when I was growing up in the 1980s, we were taught that the way to be a good person was to swear that race didn't matter, at least not anymore. We had all learned the lessons of the civil rights movement: everybody is equal, and according to the morals of the sitcoms we watched after school (*Diff'rent Strokes, Webster, Saved by the Bell*), what was racist was pretending that people were any different from one another. Furthermore, the most unracist people didn't even see race at all; they were color-blind. We now know that color-blindness is a form of racial denial that took one of the aspirations of the civil rights movement—that individuals would one day "not be judged by the color of their skin but by the content of their character"—and stripped from it any consideration of power, hierarchy, or structure. The moral logic and social appeal of color-blindness are clear, and many well-meaning people have embraced it. But when it is put into practice in a still-racist world, the result is more racism.

For two generations now, well-meaning white people have subscribed to color-blindness in an optimistic attempt to wish away the existence of structural racism. But when they do, they unwittingly align themselves with, and give mainstream cover to, a powerful movement to turn back the clock on integration and equality. What my former University of California, Berkeley, law professor Ian Haney López calls "reactionary color-blindness" has become the weapon of choice for conservatives in the courts and in politics. Racial conservatives on the Supreme Court have used the logic to rule that it's racist for communities to voluntarily integrate schools, because to do so, the government would have to "see" race to assign students. Well-funded political groups mount campaigns to forbid the government from collecting racial data because isn't that what a racist would do? Instead of being blind to race, color-blindness makes people blind to racism, unwilling to acknowledge where its effects have shaped opportunity or to use race-conscious solutions to address it.

* * *

Denial that racism still exists; denial that, even if it does exist, it's to blame for the situation at hand; denial that the problem is as bad as people of color say it is—these denials are the easy outs that the dominant white narrative offers to people. Wellesley College professor Jennifer Chudy's research finds that only one in five white Americans consistently expresses high levels of sympathy about anti-black discrimination.

Color-blindness has become a powerful weapon against progress for people of color, but as a denial mindset, it doesn't do white people any favors, either. A person who avoids the realities of racism doesn't build the crucial muscles for navigating cross-cultural tensions or recovering with grace from missteps. That person is less likely to listen deeply to unexpected ideas expressed by people from other cultures or to do the research on her own to learn about her blind spots. When that person then faces the inevitable uncomfortable racial reality—an offended coworker, a presentation about racial disparity at a PTA meeting, her inadvertent use of a stereotype—she's caught flat-footed. Denial leaves people ill prepared to function or thrive in a diverse society. It makes people less effective at collaborating with colleagues, coaching kids' sports teams, advocating for their neighborhoods, even chatting with acquaintances at social events.

Nor is denial easy to sustain. To uphold the illusion of effortless white advantage actually requires unrelenting psychological exertion. The sociologist Dr. Jennifer Mueller explains that color-blindness is a key step in "a process of knowing designed to produce not knowing surrounding white privilege, culpability, and structural white supremacy."

But it was a white poet, novelist, and farmer named Wendell Berry whose words brought home to me most poignantly the moral consequences of denial. In August 2017, I traveled to northern Kentucky to meet with a multiracial grassroots organization called Kentuckians for the Commonwealth. After a day of workshops, one of the members gave me a dog-eared copy of a 1970 book by Berry, a local hero who had grown up in rural Kentucky during the Jim Crow era. The book was called *The Hidden Wound*, and that night in my hotel room, I read it from cover to cover.

By denying the reality of racism and their own role in it, Berry explained, many white Americans have denied themselves critical self-knowledge and created a prettified and falsified version of American history for themselves to believe in, one built on the "wishful insinuation that we have done no harm." Of course, he understood the impulse of most white people—himself included—to protect themselves from "the anguish implicit in their racism."

A few years before Berry published *The Hidden Wound*, James Baldwin, as keen an observer of human behavior as there's ever been, wrote his own account of what happens when white people open their eyes to racism. "What they see is a disastrous, continuing, present condition which menaces them, and for which they bear an inescapable responsibility. But since, in the main, they seem to lack the energy to change this condition, they would rather not be reminded of it." Baldwin went on to observe that white

Americans "are dimly, or vividly, aware that the history they have fed themselves is mainly a lie, but they do not know how to release themselves from it, and they suffer enormously from the resulting personal incoherence."

Wendell Berry calls this suffering "the hidden wound." He counsels that when "you begin to awaken to the realities of what you know, you are subject to staggering recognitions of your complicity in history and in the events of your own life." Of this wound—this psychic and emotional damage that racism does to white people—he writes, "I have borne it all my life . . . always with the most delicate consideration for the pain I would feel if I were somehow forced to acknowledge it."

In a 2019 public opinion survey, majorities of both black and white people said that being black makes it more difficult to get ahead in America. Yet only 56 percent of white respondents believed the corollary: that being white helps you get ahead. And of those who recognized the obstacles black people face in terms of economic mobility, black respondents attributed this to systemic discrimination, such as having less access to good schools and high-paying jobs. White people, on the other hand, were more likely to blame problems such as the lack of good role models and family instability—group pathologies, in other words, that ultimately lay blame at the feet of black people themselves.

Morally defending your position in a racially unequal society requires the fierce protection of your self-image as a person who earns everything you receive. From the tradition that trade unions make a place for members' sons, to legacy admissions at colleges, to college students who can choose career-building but unpaid or low-paying internships because families can support them, to employers who seek "a good fit" by hiring younger versions of themselves, the deck is stacked on behalf of white people in ways that are so pervasive we rarely notice them. Within this context, many white people both resent affirmative action and imagine that it is vastly more wide-spread than it really is. The share of black and brown students at selective colleges has actually declined over thirty-five years despite stated affirmative action policies, and the overwhelmingly white categories of children of alumni, faculty, donors, or athletes made up 43 percent, for example, of students admitted to Harvard from 2010 to 2015. Meanwhile, according to a 2016 study by Harvard Business School professor Katherine DeCelles, black job applicants who removed any indications of their race from their résumés were significantly more likely to advance to an interview. Many other studies bear out similar findings, including an economic research paper that traced improved job prospects to whether applicants had names like Greg or Emily as opposed to Lakisha or Jamal, and a sociological study in New York City that found that "black applicants were half as likely as equally qualified whites to receive a callback or job offer."

Still, the idea that people of color are taking jobs from white people is another zero-sum belief that lumbers on from era to era. As Ronald, a middle-aged white man from Buffalo, New York, told the Whiteness Project, "I think affirmative action was nice. It had its time, but I think that time is over with. Are we going to keep this up another one hundred fifty years? 'Oh, we gotta have so many

Asians in the fire department, we gotta have so many blacks in the fire department.' . . . The white guys will never have a chance to be a fireman or a cop anymore." Although using such numerical quotas to achieve affirmative action in employment was outlawed in 1978 by the Supreme Court, Ronald's grievance is evergreen, as is his certainty that white guys getting all the public service jobs was the natural order of things, not its own form of white affirmative action.

BE SCARED FOR THEM

None of these economic resentments and justifications has the life-or-death consequences of the most powerful morally inverting force in our society: white fear of people of color, particularly black people. In the American moral logic—and, increasingly, with "Stand Your Ground" laws, in the legal system—when you fear someone, no matter how objectively real the threat, you can be justified in doing them harm. If you have a badge, that moral and legal license has been seemingly without limit. In 2019, police officers nationwide shot and killed more than one thousand people; there were only twenty-seven days that year when no civilians died from police shootings. Black people constituted 28 percent of those killed, more than twice our presence in the population. Although 1.3 times more likely than white people to be unarmed, black people were three times more likely to be killed by police. Indigenous Americans are killed by police at shocking rates as high as or higher than those for African Americans.

But we may actually have reached the moral limit. For over nine minutes, people around the world watched a white police officer kneel on the neck of George Floyd, a black man in Minneapolis, until he died. In his dying moments, Floyd called out for his "Mama," who had already died two years before. White Americans had seen and explained away videos of police killings before, but this was too much. After months in isolation and fear from a callously mismanaged pandemic that disproportionately sickened and killed people of color, it was too much. On the heels of the murder of Ahmaud Arbery, chased by white men in a pickup truck while jogging and then gunned down, it was too much. After the police killed Breonna Taylor, an emergency medical technician in Louisville, Kentucky, who had been asleep in her own bed before a botched raid, it was too much. An estimated 15 to 26 million people demonstrated to protest police brutality in the summer of 2020, a tidal wave of recognition about the reality of systemic anti-blackness that prompted dozens of laws reforming police practices.

Maureen Wanket is one of the many white people who has joined the Black Lives Matter movement. She's a middle-aged teacher who once worked at Sacramento High, the school where a young man named Stephon Clark used to play football and ace his first-period history tests. On March 18, 2018, two Sacramento police officers responding to a vandalism call shot at Stephon twenty times, killing him before identifying themselves. Many of those rounds were fired into Stephon's back. The twenty-two-year-old father of two was killed in his grandmother's backyard. The only "weapon" police found was a cell phone. Yet the officers faced no criminal charges because they could claim that they had been in fear for their lives.

In the days following the shooting, when Sacramento was roiled by protests and recriminations, one of Maureen's colleagues at the majority-white Catholic school where she now teaches approached her with sympathy. "You care more because you . . . taught there at Sac High, and so it's like when someone visits the zoo, they get really used to the animals."

The woman's words knocked Maureen breathless. Recalling that moment, she said, "This woman has been so kind to me since I first started working there. She thinks she's being cool." Yet she was likening black students to animals and suggesting that Maureen needed a reason to care about them.

This wasn't the first time Maureen encountered fellow white people who assumed she shared their racial fears. She recalls with overwhelming fondness her years teaching at Sacramento High, the public charter school whose students were all from working-class backgrounds and mostly African American, with a small percentage of Hmong and Latinx kids. "These were the best students of my career," she said. "If I gave the students something to read, they read it in three days. I would sometimes plan a lesson [unit] to go on for four or five weeks, and they were done in two weeks and wanted to write the paper because they were excited." Yet the most frequent question Maureen received from her white friends about the school and its students was "Are you scared?"

Her response: "Scared of what? Don't be scared of black kids. Be scared *for* them."

* * *

In one year, white people called the police on black people for engaging in such menacing behaviors as napping in a common room of their own dorm; standing in a doorway to wait out the rain; cashing a check in a bank; using a coupon in a store; waiting for a friend in a coffee shop; and (that most American of activities) going door to door to canvass voters. And in a taped encounter that went viral in 2020, Christian Cooper was bird-watching in Central Park when Amy Cooper (no relation) called the police on him for asking her to follow the law by leashing her dog.

Where does this fear come from? Segregation breeds unfamiliarity; strategic disinvestment of many neighborhoods of color makes them economically depressed and appear to many white people like no-go zones. Then there's the news. Tuning in to your local news, you could easily reach the conclusion that far fewer white people than black people engage in criminal behavior, even though the opposite is true. Among those in the United States arrested for criminal activity, the vast majority, 69 percent, is white. Yet white people constitute only about 28 percent of the people who appear on crime reports on TV news, while black people are dramatically overrepresented. Yes, violent crime rates are higher in disinvested neighborhoods of color than in well-resourced white enclaves, but once you control for poverty, the difference disappears. Crime victimization is as prevalent in poor white communities as poor black communities; it's similar in rural poor areas and urban poor ones. In addition, less policing in middle-income and wealthy neighborhoods means that their violent crimes often go unreported.

White fear isn't just determinative of one-on-one interactions;

it's a social force that can be manipulated through the media and politics to change voting and economic behavior. At the start of the summer of mass demonstrations against police violence in 2020, the moral contours of the struggle were crystal clear to the majority of Americans. A sea change in public opinion happened virtually overnight, and 95 percent of the counties where Black Lives Matter demonstrations were held were majority white. But as law enforcement escalated against some of the bigger protests, the media coverage was drawn to scenes of conflict. Right-wing social media began to proliferate images of chaos, and the White House Twitter account rhetoric about "law and order" increased. A new political narrative emerged: the protestors are dangerous, in the wrong, and menacing. The specter of violence in the streets—even, as it was, between unarmed demonstrators and militarized police—managed to turn white public opinion as the summer wore on.

By early August, pollsters were showing a roughly even split between people who believed that the protests were mostly peaceful and those who believed they were mostly violent. As a result, support for the goals of the movement was down among conflicted, or swing, voters by 28 percent from June. "I am pretty moderate in my views, but I believe in law and order," said a typical white male focus group participant. The perception was that violence was as common as ordinary protest activity, but the most complete record of the summer 2020 racial justice protests shows that 93 percent of the events were peaceful, with no conflict, violence, or property destruction. As overblown as the fears might have been, the impact on solidarity with black people was real. The share of white Americans who said that racism was a big problem fell from 45 percent in June in the aftermath of George Floyd's death to just 33 percent in August, an abandonment of the 75 percent of black Americans whose concern about racism remained constant throughout.

THE POWER OF PROJECTION

My mother, who was born in 1950, grew up with a healthy fear of white people. A white person would have been able to roll up beside her in a truck and kidnap her, and probably nothing would have happened to him. A white person could have denied her a house—and did—and nothing happened to them. For the life of her, she could not understand why white people always professed to be so afraid of people of color.

"It's so strange," my mother used to tell me, "because we're the ones who live in terror of what white people can do with impunity."

It dawned on me as a teenager that many white people must fear, at some deep level, that given half a chance, people of color would do to them what they have long been doing to us. Later I would learn that this dynamic of assigning others your own worst attributes has a name: projection. The legal scholar Richard Thompson Ford writes, "In order for the concept of a white race to exist, there must be a black race which is everything the white race is not." It's not real, of course. We are all complex individuals. But the total white power over laws and culture has mapped these ideas onto our minds.

I grew up unwittingly devouring tales of racist projection. My dad would take me to watch the epic, sprawling Westerns I loved on the big screen whenever there was a revival: *The Searchers; The Good, the Bad and the Ugly; Stagecoach.* They were morality plays, all of them, and they taught generations of Americans not just about "how the West was won," but also about good guys and bad guys. There was just one problem: in a land where white Americans had committed one of history's greatest genocides, the white cowboys were the stoic heroes; the interchangeable, whooping Indians, the villains.

White fear can exist only in "a world turned upside down," writes Abraham Lateiner, a white man born into wealth who has become an activist for equality. "Because white people stole two continents and two hundred years of the backbreaking labor of millions, race reassures us that blackness is related to thievery," he writes. "Because white men have raped black and Brown women with impunity for centuries, race comforts us with the lie that it's black masculinity that is defined by hypersexual predation. Because white people penned black people in the 'ghetto' via redlining, race tells us that this 'ghetto' is an indictment of black pathology. People of color weren't the ones who created whiteness or violated my spirit with it. That was my own people. That is my peers. That is me, too."

One summer day in 2018, I was getting a ride from one interview stop to another with a white retiree I'll call Ken. The miles passed beneath the tires of his white SUV, and an oldies station played quietly beneath our chatter. The conversation turned to Colin Kaepernick, the professional football player who knelt during the playing of the national anthem to protest police brutality against black people. Ken had spent much of the car ride telling me how much he hated the racism and police brutality that seemed to be on the rise in the country and that he supported Black Lives Matter, so I expected him to agree with me when I praised Kaepernick's courage. Instead, he told me he felt attacked by this symbolic act.

"I don't understand," I said. "You agree that cops getting away with killing unarmed black people is wrong." To me, that put Ken on Kaepernick's side. Why would he feel attacked by someone with whom he agreed?

"I do. I do," he said, nodding, thoughtful. Then he smacked his hand on the steering wheel. I swiveled in my seat to stare at him. "But it's like he's using a shotgun instead of a rifle," he said, "it's spraying too wide and hitting innocent bystanders."

I turned my gaze back to the road, unnerved by the way his analogy placed a gun in the hand of a kneeling, peaceful protestor. My thoughts were roiling. Who were the innocent bystanders? Not the black victims of police violence. Not the football players whose silent protest fell squarely in the democratic tradition. No, the innocents in Ken's mind were white people like him, people who might not approve of police officers killing the black citizens they were sworn to protect but who did not think it was fair to be reminded of those killings during a football game. The innocents were those who found more outrage in the act of protesting violence than in the violence itself. And why did Ken feel personally attacked—wounded, even? What part of Ken was so tightly woven into the flag that he perceived a protest against American injustice as a protest against him, even when he agreed with the message?

I found it hard to relate. I didn't share Ken's reverence for the pageantry, the performative love of country with no room for the truth about that country. But I do love America. I love its ideals: equality, freedom, liberty, justice. It's what Langston Hughes meant in 1936 when he wrote, "Let America be America again—The land that never has been yet—And yet must be." It is how Dr. King could say that his dream was rooted in the American Dream. It's why Kaepernick's protest says, "Not so fast. This America isn't living up to the bargain, so I won't shake hands until she does."

Wanting someone to stand for the national anthem rather than stand up for justice means loving the symbol more than what it symbolizes. Ken's attachment to American innocence made him take the side that opposed his own stated beliefs, just as our nation has done time and time again. It's the moral upside down of racism that simultaneously extolls American virtues in principle and rejects them in practice.

America's symbols were not designed to represent people of color or to speak to us—nonetheless, the ideals they signify have been more than slogans; they have meant life or death for us. Equality, freedom, liberty, justice—who could possibly love those ideals more than those denied them? African Americans became a people here, and our people sacrificed every last imaginable thing to America's becoming. The promise of this country has been enough to rend millions of immigrants from their homes, and for today's mostly of-color immigrants, it's still enough, despite persecution, detention, and death, to keep them dreaming of finding freedom here. The profound love for America's ideals should unite all who call it home, of every color—and yet America has lied to her white children for centuries, offering them songs about freedom instead of the liberation of truth.

THE SPIRITUAL COSTS OF RACISM

As I tried to figure out how the country's moral progress had stalled, I finally realized that I should ask people whose job—or, rather, calling—it is to guide us morally. But there was a quandary, and that is the role that the largest religion in America has played in perpetuating American racism—and the way racial hierarchy seeps into religious institutions of all faiths. When the Rev. Dr. Martin Luther King Jr. was leading the Birmingham antisegregation campaign in 1963, a group of white clergy signed on to a letter urging him to stop. The civil rights activists, the white clergy said, were breaking the law with their nonviolent demonstrations, and so were in the wrong. From jail, Dr. King famously wrote, "I am sorry that your statement did not express a similar concern for the conditions that brought the demonstrations into being. . . . We will have to repent in this generation not merely for the hateful words and actions of the bad people but for the appalling silence of the good people."

The African American Christian tradition is almost synonymous with social justice in America, from abolition to the civil rights movement to contemporary leaders like Rev. William Barber, who led the Moral Mondays Movement in North Carolina and now leads a revived Poor People's Campaign. But white Christian leadership is still grappling with its role in acknowledging and dismantling racism. To talk to one of those leaders, I visited an Evangelical church in Chicago called River City, founded by a pastor named Daniel Hill. I sat in the back of the large, unadorned room for services so as to observe and not intrude, but this inadvertently put me in the families and children section. I was surrounded by row after row of the largest group of interracial families I'd ever seen in one room. I asked Pastor Daniel about it after services. River City is a strict Evangelical church in that its congregants believe in the literal word of God as recorded in the Bible—and that Word, Pastor Daniel told me, compelled them to create a deliberately multicultural church.

"Well, Revelation 7:9 is a vision of heaven that is every tongue and every tribe that God's ever created." Furthermore, Pastor Daniel told me, "It's impossible to have a meaningful relationship with Jesus and not care about the evil in our day and age. The ideology of white supremacy is, if not the premier form of evil, it's at least one of the clearest forms of evil on a large scale in our day and age." So he uses his ministry to teach the antiracist lessons of the Bible, confront white privilege in Christianity, and create a multiracial church in the heart of segregated Chicago.

But Pastor Daniel and River City are the exceptions to the rule, and it took a conversation with someone I've known for years, Reverend Jim Wallis, to explain why. Jim is a white Evangelical minister in his seventies with the warm blue eyes and smiling face of a Little League coach (which he has been for more than twenty seasons). In a conspiratorial tone over a long phone call, Jim told me the story of ruffling feathers at a gathering of the small circle of primarily white men who head the major Christian denominations in America.

"Now," Rev. Wallis told the men, walking around the circle and making eye contact with each one, "you all have been told or taught or learned how slavery was common, and slavery was all over the world. But we uniquely did something. We Christians, in fact—British and American—were the ones who decided that we couldn't do to Indigenous people and kidnapped Africans what we were doing, if they were indeed people made in the image of God.

"So, we said they weren't. They weren't humans made in the image of God. What we did is we threw away *Imago Dei*. We threw it away to justify what we're doing. . . . white supremacy was America's original sin. . . . At the heart of the sin was a lie," he said.

On the phone with me, Jim Wallis's voice grew deeper and fuller as he leaned into his point. "As long as white people—even, you know, good-hearted, well-meaning, progressive white people—think that the issue of race is mostly about people of color and minorities and what has happened to them and what happens to them that we could help with—as long as that's the mindset, they're still stuck," he told me.

And they will remain stuck "until we understand as white people that the problem of racism is about us." Jim doesn't take this call lightly. He says that "to confront this and change this is necessary for our salvation. To confront racism is not a question of charity or virtue for white Christians," he declared. "This is to save our souls."

The same way that Pastor Daniel preaches about the many

antiracist messages in the New Testament, Rabbi Felicia Sol, senior rabbi at the large New York City Jewish congregation B'nai Jeshurun, revealed how the spiritual imperative against racism is located deep in the foundational texts and stories of her faith. "For the leitmotif of the Jewish tradition, we have a redemption narrative at our core. The Exodus from Egypt is a Jewish story. And that story has been utilized for liberation movements throughout history." But, she said, many religious scholars consider that "redemption isn't a miracle. It's actually built into the structure of the world. . . . And therefore, racism is an impediment to the structure of the world, of a redeemed world.

"The story goes that God was trying to make the world, and the world wouldn't stand up until *teshuvah*—'repentance'—was created. . . . And I find that a deeply compelling narrative. The structure of the world understands . . . it would have to repair itself at its core. But that repair is on us, you know."

Rabbi Sol made the religious case that racism cuts both ways. "Racism actually has a dehumanizing aspect not only for those who experience racism, but [also for] those who perpetuate it. . . . Jewish tradition articulates . . . that everyone is stamped in the image of God." And in some Jewish traditions, she said, "there's a notion that God is not a hierarchical God, but that God is the oneness of all of us. . . . There's no difference between me and God. It's all the same. God is one. And so, racism is another way that divides that divine connection . . . because then we're not only inflicting pain on others, but we're maligning our purity."

Islam also espouses a theology of equality and fraternity among all humankind, and certain interpretations of its teachings about self-reliance and equality have appealed to many generations of African Americans, including but by no means limited to civil rights icons like Malcolm X. Among non-black Muslim Americans with immigrant backgrounds, the shared experiences of suspicion and surveillance—especially after 9/11—have been a source of solidarity with antiracist struggles. When I spoke with Zaheer Ali, a Brooklyn-based oral historian, he pointed to the line in the Quran in which Allah proclaims to humankind that "we . . . made you into nations and tribes [so] that you may know each other, not that you may despise each other." Ali was born in Trinidad, the Caribbean island where the descendants of Indian laborers (Muslim, Hindu, and Sikh) and enslaved Africans commingled for over a century, and he has spent much of his career documenting the oral history of American Muslims. He painted a complicated picture for me of a religious doctrine that was profoundly antihierarchical and has attracted many black Americans away from the Christianity so entangled with white supremacy and slavery. But he also talked about the anti-blackness that many South Asian, Persian, and Arab Muslim immigrants adopt as part of their assimilation process in America.

Just hours after my conversation with Zaheer, Minneapolis police officers killed George Floyd. Zaheer wrote me an email the day after the city of Minneapolis and the country erupted. "That it was a Muslim/Arab-owned store that called the police on George Floyd throws some of what we discussed into sharper relief (and even greater urgency): the need to speak to anti-black racism within

Muslim communities." I had taken note of that fact as well, but replied asking him if he'd seen the news story of a local Bangladeshi Muslim family whose business, a restaurant named Gandhi Mahal, a few doors down from the Third Precinct of the Minneapolis Police Department, had caught fire in the protests. After losing his family's business, the father, Ruhel Islam, reportedly said, "Let my building burn. Justice needs to be served." I had read Mr. Islam's next words with tears in my eyes: "We can rebuild a building, but we cannot rebuild a human." Racism taught generations of white Americans that we were no more than property. I didn't know how much I needed to hear someone say that even if it cost them everything, they knew better.

For all the differences among the world's major religions, they all hold compassion and human interconnectedness as central values; they all subscribe to a sacred vision of a world without racism. As I traveled the country engaging with people about the costs of racism, I often began our conversations discussing laws and policies, wealth and income—but in the end, many of the talks settled into a quiet, personal place. People brown, black, and white revealed a moment of confession, of frustration, or of hope, and it all came from an emotional, even spiritual sense that this just isn't how we're supposed to be. It made me think more deeply about my own spiritual beliefs. I believe in a divine force to which we are all connected, and I admire the rituals and community-building that organized religion offers, but I didn't grow up as a churchgoer. (My mother, a deeply spiritual woman and a feminist, could never really accept a religion that figured the divine creator as male.) Yet I realized that I pursue my professional calling not only to improve our economy, but also out of a belief in the unseen: a promised land of a caring, just society. Across my conversations for this book, I heard a unified yearning for a society like that.

Racism destroys every path to that promised land, for all of us. As Wendell Berry writes, "If white people have suffered less obviously from racism than black people, they have nevertheless suffered greatly; the cost has been greater perhaps than we can yet know."

CHAPTER 10

THE SOLIDARITY DIVIDEND

I PARKED IN A VACANT LOT ON THE SOUTHERNMOST END OF Lisbon Street, the main thoroughfare of Lewiston, Maine. The street dead-ends near the old canal, built to power the cotton mills that made Lewiston one of the more prosperous towns in America in the late 1800s. The mills, the prosperity, even much of the canal, are now gone. "Dying mill towns" like Lewiston have been ground zero for propagation of the zero-sum story: Lewiston was once great for its white residents and began to fall apart in the same era when civil rights were on the rise and the country grew more diverse. *Progress for people of color means a loss for white people.* But this equation adds up only if you leave out the decisions by corporate employers to seek cheaper labor, or the trade policies that were the final death knell in the 1990s and 2000s.

Maine is the state with the whitest and oldest population in the country, whose children are the least likely in the country to have a classmate of color. The state ranks among the top ten in opioid deaths. From 2011 to 2019, the state's right-wing governor, Paul LePage, campaigned and governed on rhetoric about illegal immigrants on welfare and drug-dealing people of color. Meanwhile, he vetoed Medicaid expansion for the working class five times and delivered large tax cuts for the wealthy. I traveled to Lewiston because of the ways its residents are especially vulnerable to the zero-sum story, but also because of a promising phenomenon I saw signs of about ten minutes into my walk up the town's main street.

At the beginning of my walk, many of the buildings I saw—richly constructed nineteenth-century brick with Italianate moldings—stood stately and vacant, with neatly boarded-up windows on the ground floor. Here and there, a storefront lawyer's office appeared, with a couple of desks, needing far less space than it had; a pawnshop complex occupied much of an entire block. But once I crossed Chestnut Street, Lisbon Street came alive. Windows were suddenly stacked high with goods, framed by posters for mobile wire transfers and prepaid cards. One store had an arresting display of caftans and hijabs in bright coordinated colors. Another, next to the shadow of a faded old grocery store sign, had a sign reading MOGADISHU BUSINESS CENTER. The shop offered groceries, a restaurant, money transfer, a seamstress, a tax preparer, cleaning services, halal meat—and sweet, strong coffee, as I learned when I stopped in to fuel up.

The door chimes marked my departure from the street into a

warm, fragrant, and music-filled shop. In the aisle near a wall of bulk spices, I saw two men and a young boy speaking in a language I recognized as Somali. As I ordered my coffee from the young hijab-wearing woman behind the counter, we chatted about how long she'd been in Maine (seven years), the weather (what good comes from complaining?), and after my first sip, the spices in my coffee (a secret blend, but yes, cardamom). I exited the Somali shop and looked around at the white and black residents on the street with a smile. Maybe these somewhat accidental neighbors were destined to create another story, a different formula from the zero sum, one more fitting for our future as a nation of many.

I turned off Lisbon to enter the historic City Hall. Through the open doors, I saw a stately marble hallway flanked by large portraits of every mayor in Lewiston history. I understood the reason for the tribute, but I also recognized, from so many institutions I'd been in, how it feels to be a person who doesn't look like the images on the walls, which were almost all of white men. It's hard not to get the message that this place—no matter who occupies it at the moment—belongs to them, not you. Then, down the middle of that long hallway came bounding a man as animated as the portraits were still: Phil Nadeau, the deputy city administrator. He greeted me warmly and showed me into an office decked with maps and memorabilia. My eye immediately went to the famous photograph of Muhammad Ali in the boxing ring, lording it over the knocked-down Sonny Liston. I was shocked when Nadeau told me that the heavyweight title fight had happened just around the corner in Lewiston, in a youth hockey rink in 1965.

Unlike the elected and largely symbolic mayors, Nadeau was an urban planner appointed to run the day-to-day nuts and bolts of the town. He explained Lewiston's decline in blunt terms: "It was a one-and-a-half-industry town. Come the sixties and seventies, when it's pretty clear [the jobs] are going, there's little that you can do to stop it. There were a variety of things that we tried to help those businesses remain viable. But it was a losing battle against a global economy." Soon, everything that was once manufactured in Lewiston would be made in the American South with cheaper labor, and eventually in China and Southeast Asia. By the 2000s, the loss of jobs had created a vicious circle: as young people left to find work, there was nobody to work the few service-sector jobs that remained in the wake of shuttered factories. Then, with the town losing population year after year, it was impossible to attract new employers. Lisbon Street, once the second-biggest commercial district in the state, began to show as many vacant windows as store displays. When Nadeau moved to his position in Lewiston city government in the early 2000s, it became clear to him that only one thing would save the town: new people.

"Maine is the oldest state in the country. One of only two now in the country, Maine and West Virginia, where deaths now exceed births. None of this is good news."

I asked him why getting new people actually mattered to those who stayed; how did he counter the idea that newcomers were just competing for dwindling resources? He shook his head emphatically. "You can't convince businesses to either expand or move into your state or into your community if the bodies aren't there. These companies know this about Maine. But here's the city of Lewiston bucking that trend."

The secret to Lewiston's success was something of an accident: in the early 1990s, the US government accepted thousands of refugees from the Somali Civil War and resettled many to the Atlanta suburbs of Georgia. Word of mouth got some to Portland, and then to Lewiston, where the quiet streets offered more peace and the low rents more security. Family by family, Lewiston's refugee population grew. Soon it wasn't just Somalis but many other African refugees, from the Congo, Chad, Djibouti, and Sudan.

"The refugee arrivals . . . are filling apartments that were vacant for a long time. They're filling storefronts on Lisbon Street that were vacant for a long time. They're contributing to the economy." Phil Nadeau is passionate about the value of the "new Mainers," as he calls them, to the revitalization of Lewiston. He boasts that while other Maine small towns had plummeting real estate values, fleeing young people, and shuttering schools, Lewiston is building new schools—and creating the jobs that come with that. Though Phil also credits good regional planning and maintenance of the historic assets—the infrastructure built nearly a century ago, the hundreds of thousands of square feet of factories that have not become blighted—he simply can't say enough about the benefit of migration to small towns like his. A bipartisan think tank calculated that Maine's African immigrant households contributed $194 million in state and local taxes in 2018.

When I met Nadeau, he was in his last weeks on a job that has taken him through multiple administrations of elected mayors who, to put it mildly, haven't shared his enthusiasm for the changing face of Lewiston. But Phil has seen the economic fortunes of the town reverse, and for a city planner, there's nothing controversial about that. He plans to spend his retirement crossing the country to share the good word about how immigration can be a win-win for locals. "I could talk about it all day long." Phil sat back in his chair and allowed a broad smile to finish his point.

NEW PEOPLE

Lewiston is not alone in this new wave of new people; for the past twenty years, Latinx, African, and Asian immigrants have been re-populating small towns across America. Pick a state, and you'll find this story in one corner or another. Kennett Square, Pennsylvania, is now 50 percent Latinx, mostly from Mexico, and it's a community given new life by the families of migrant workers at the local mushroom farms. In Storm Lake, Iowa, the elementary school is 90 percent children of color. Towns across the Texas Panhandle have been drying up and losing population for years, but the potato farming stronghold of Dalhart grew by 7 percent from 1990 to 2016 because of Latinx families. Low-paid farm and food process-ing work is what draws foreign-born people to these small towns at first, for sure. But once there, immigrants have, as European im-migrants did a century ago, started businesses, gained education, and participated in civic life (though the Europeans' transition to whiteness offered a glide path to the middle class unavailable to immigrants of color today). Even in the face of anti-immigrant policies and the absence of vehicles for mobility such as unions and housing subsidies, today's immigrants of color are revitalizing rural America. A study of more than 2,600 rural communities found that over the three decades after 1990, two-thirds lost population. However, immigration helped soften the blow in the majority of these places, and among the areas that gained population, one in five owes the entirety of its growth to immigration. In the decade after 2000, people of color made up nearly 83 percent of the growth in rural population in America.

In many of these communities, longtime residents—who are overwhelmingly white—have chosen not to feel threatened by these new people of color. The temptation is there, and the encouragement from anti-immigrant politicians is certainly there, but the growth and prosperity the new people bring give the lie to the zero-sum model. Locals know that the alternative to new people is compounding losses: factories, residents, then the hospitals and schools and the attendant jobs. So, the residents are putting aside prejudices in order to grow their hometowns, together. If they don't, wrote Art Cullen, the local newspaper editor in Storm Lake, Iowa, "there will be nobody left to turn out the lights by 2050" in towns like his. "Asians and Africans and Latinos are our lifeline," he declared flatly in 2018.

These small-town success stories are full of local gestures, both big and small, to integrate the newcomers, ranging from free ESL classes to community college partnerships to help new immigrants get degrees. One of these gestures changed the life of Lewiston resident Cecile Thornton, but it wasn't she who offered the education to her new neighbors; they gave it to her. A quarter of Maine citizens, like Cecile, have Franco-American heritage—mostly descendants of French-speaking Canadian immigrants who came to work the cotton mills and shoe factories a hundred years ago—but only 3 percent of the state speaks French regularly at home, and Cecile is among the many "Francos" who have lost their French. Cecile was born in 1955 to French-speaking parents and did her best to forget the French she'd learned at the dinner table, escaping to the living room once the family got a TV set and repeating the words of Walter Cronkite to learn how "real" Americans spoke. The "Francos" were the butt of schoolyard jokes, so by high school, Cecile made sure to suppress her accent altogether and held on to very few words of her native French.

When I met her, she'd also lost the closeness of her family. "All of my family is away, including my kids," she told me. "They're all out of state. And my aunts and uncles, my parents, all of those people are dead." The kind of isolation that Cecile faced when she retired to an empty home in Lewiston has become a growing epidemic among older people in rural and suburban America. The US surgeon general Vivek Murthy has linked it to the "diseases of despair" that are disproportionately haunting white Americans facing economic decline: alcoholism, drug abuse, and suicide. Social isolation has been found to lower life expectancy by a degree comparable to smoking almost a pack of cigarettes a day.

But a few years ago, Cecile made a decision that turned her story around. She got in her car to drive to the Franco Center downtown. She went looking for a connection—to other people, to her community, to the language that had filled her home as a child. What she found on the first day at the center, however, was a roomful of elderly people who had long ago traded away French for belonging—to become no longer "Francos," but simply, white. It was a cultural assimilation that happened in time to every group of white-skinned immigrants in the nineteenth and early twentieth centuries, from the Italians to the Poles. What America offered for the price of assimilation was inclusion in the pool of whites-only benefits that shaped the middle class, but we don't talk much about what they left behind.

The Franco Center had a rule: put a quarter in a jar every time you spoke English. The maximum penalty was one dollar, though, so when Cecile looked around, all the tables had jars full of dollars and conversations carrying on in English. She couldn't hide her disappointment: even here at the Franco Center, her community's language seemed lost. In her isolation, the idea of reclaiming her French had become a lifeline, so she wasn't giving up—she found the most talkative person in the room and complained. He told her, "You should go to the French Club at Hillview." Hillview is a subsidized housing project in Lewiston. When Cecile arrived at one o'clock on a weekday afternoon for the advertised French Club, she was shocked to see that she was the only white person there.

"I didn't even know at the time that we had Africans in the city who spoke French. I had no clue, none." The first man she spoke with, Edho, had just followed his wife and children to Lewiston from Congo. After a timid "Bonjour" from Cecile, she and Edho launched into the longest French conversation Cecile had had since her childhood, with Edho helping her recall long-gone words and phrases. By the end of the first session, she was exhausted but thrilled. "Just as an interested and curious person, when I was meeting these people, I just fell in love with them." She laughs, knowing what that sounds like. "Not that I really fell in love with them, but I felt like I belonged with them."

Over the next year, Cecile would make the Francophone African community of Lewiston the center of her life. When she noticed that it became hard for Hillview folks to attend French Club once they enrolled in community college downtown or got a job, she launched a new French Club, at the more convenient Franco Center downtown, but she heavily recruited her new African friends to come. With Cecile's encouragement, soon the two populations of French speakers were mixing: elderly white Mainers with halting vocabularies learning from new black Mainers who spoke fluently. Francophone Africans like Edho, once seen as strange folks from far away, were now teachers. Today, Cecile volunteers to help asylum seekers, doing winter coat drives and connecting new arrivals to services, but she'd be the first to say that what she gives pales in comparison with what she has received.

After my conversation with Phil Nadeau, I went back to Lisbon Street to the Mogadishu Business Center to talk with one of the owners, Said, a gregarious Somali man with soft brown eyes. Said told me that one of the first white Mainers to venture into the store was a woman named Brenda, who was drawn by the clothes hanging in the front. She asked so many questions that it became evident that she was a skilled seamstress who had been out of work for some time. She struck up a rapport with the store's other owner, Said's wife, known to all as Mama Shukri. Mama Shukri offered Brenda a job repairing the hijabs and caftans people would bring into the shop. Said explained, "And then she started making new clothes after that."

My eyes got wider. "So, Brenda started making African clothes?"

Said nodded matter-of-factly. "Yeah. She's very good."

He told me more stories about integration going well at the person-to-person level, including in the Lewiston Blue Devils soccer team, which African immigrant kids from six countries had led to three years of state championships. White Mainers and African Mainers doing business together was going well, too, he said. It's the government he worries about. In fact, Lewiston has been governed by mayors using harsh anti-immigrant rhetoric for all of the twenty years that Somalis have been present. After the first group of families arrived in Lewiston by word of mouth, then-Mayor Laurier Raymond Jr. wrote an open letter saying that the town was full, even though much of downtown lay vacant. "This large number of new arrivals cannot continue without negative results for all," Raymond wrote. The letter became a rallying cry for white supremacists, who descended on the town for a march soon after. Republican governor Paul LePage won his elections campaigning against welfare, suggesting that immigrants were stealing resources from the local taxpayers. Said shook his head. "So, [the mayor] is going to a lectern and saying, 'Oh, because of the Somalis, we are going to cut the welfare. Because these people, they're coming here only for welfare.'"

His eyes got a little distant, as they did when he was talking about home. "In central and south[ern] Africa, there's a saying: 'When election day comes, keep your knife close.' That's when the problems happen, especially inter-clan problems. But once the election is gone, people are normal. Everyone is looking for his life. They are trading with each other, friends getting married together. But the one day election comes, the knives are out. The politicians will try to separate us."

The politicians will try to separate us. The people I met—Phil, Cecile, Said with his coworker Brenda—belonged to a beachhead of solidarity amid a surge in xenophobia pushed relentlessly by politicians in Lewiston and across the country. The faith that the Lewiston people I met had in the idea of different cultures not only coexisting but thriving through their differences didn't come from theory or ideology; it came from lived experience. Each of them had had a reason to roll up their sleeves and put in the time to make some part of their community work better, and in so doing, they had bettered themselves. But the resistance of many white Mainers to new people isn't about just dollars and cents, if we're honest. It's also about the fear of a loss of community, of identity, of home. It was striking to me that what old Mainers were worried about losing is something that, by definition, the new Mainers have *actually* lost: home. And for people like Cecile and Brenda, cross-cultural friendships have given them a deeper sense of community than they ever had before.

FIVE DISCOVERIES

My journey across the US from California to Mississippi to Maine, tallying the costs of racism, has led me to five discoveries about how we can prosper together:

- The first is that we have reached the productive and moral limit of the zero-sum economic model that was crafted in the cradle of the United States. We have no choice but to start aiming for a **Solidarity Dividend**.

- The second is that the quickest way to get there is to **refill the pool of public goods**, for everyone. When our nation had generous public benefits, they were the springboard for a thriving middle class—but they were narrowly designed to serve white and soon-to-be-white Americans.

- Third, because of that, our people are not all standing at the same depths today, so we must resist the temptation to use universal instruments to attain universal ends. When it comes to designing solutions, **one size has never fit all**. Everywhere that I found white people paying the spillover costs of racism, I also found that, without exception, their coworkers and neighbors of color were paying even more, in lost wealth, health, and often lives. Getting white support to address those different levels of need, and to acknowledge the racism that caused those differences, is never easy—particularly when the zero-sum mental model turns every concession into a threat of loss.

- That's why uprooting the zero sum is so essential, as is embedding in its place the value that I found radiating out of the people who had the biggest impact on me and their communities: the knowledge that **we truly do need each other**.

- The fifth and final discovery is that we've got to get on the same page before we can turn it. We've tried a do-it-yourself approach to writing the racial narrative about America, but the forces selling denial, ignorance, and projection have succeeded in robbing us of our own shared history—both the pain and the resilience. It's time to tell the truth, with a nationwide process that enrolls all of us in setting the facts straight so that we can move forward with **a new story**, together.

The mounting challenges we face in society are going to require strength and scale that none of us can achieve on her own. The crises of climate change, inequality, pandemics, and mass involuntary movements of people are already here, and in the United States, each has exposed the poverty of our public capacity to prevent and react. Save for the ultrawealthy, we're all living at the bottom of the drained pool now. The refusal to share across race has created a society with nothing left for itself. With falling support for government over the past fifty years have come falling support for taxes, a brain drain from the public sector, and a failure to add to (or even steward) the infrastructure investments of the early twentieth century.

We have to refill the pool. Some restoration of public goods will be relatively straightforward, like rebuilding the fifty-year-old dams that are failing just in time for climate change to send heavier rains, or laying new pipes to replace the ones leaching toxins into our drinking water. We know how to do that; we've just lost the will. I'll acknowledge a bigger problem with the progressive vision for more robust government: we've let slip our capacity to deliver services with efficiency and skill. The old adage goes that poor people get poor services, and as we've ratcheted down the income level for government benefits over the past fifty years and squeezed public payrolls, the experience of dealing with the government has become increasingly frustrating and negative. Just ask the millions of people who applied for pandemic-related unemployment insurance from state agencies stripped by years of Republican budget cuts and who were still waiting months later; the graduates who were unable to get the public service loan forgiveness they'd organized their careers around due to technicalities; or the voters who navigated a maze of requirements to get a ballot and vote. Refilling the pool will require us to believe in government so much that we hold it to the highest standard of excellence and commit our generation's best and brightest to careers designing public goods instead of photo-sharing apps.

When we do, the potential is boundless.

* * *

The hundreds of conversations I had on my journey convinced me that we can't each do it on our own. We need a national effort, rooted in community, one that brings us together and has the full backing of the body that has kept us apart: the US government.

A model for such a process began locally, in 2017, when fourteen communities across the country launched efforts known as Truth, Racial Healing and Transformation (TRHT). The next year, the American Association of Colleges and Universities did the same, and by 2018, twenty-four college campuses had TRHT centers. On June 4, 2020, after a week of nationwide protests sparked by the brutal police killing of George Floyd, members of the US House of Representatives led by Rep. Barbara Lee (D-CA) introduced a resolution urging the establishment of a US TRHT Commission. The TRHT framework was developed in 2016 with the input of a group of over 175 experts convened by the W. K. Kellogg Foundation.

To launch a Truth, Racial Healing and Transformation effort, community leaders must gather a representative group of people, both demographically and in terms of the sectors in the community. The framework involves a process of relationship-building and healing by sharing personal stories about race and racism, but it doesn't just help people "talk about race"—TRHT groups also identify community decisions that have created hierarchy in three areas: law, separation, and the economy. Bridging the distance between the individual stories and the desired policy change is narrative change, accomplished by identifying manifestations of the belief in human hierarchy in our stories, be they school curricula or media portrayals or monuments, and replacing them with "complete and accurate stories that honor the full complexity of our humanity as the country forges a more equitable future." The TRHT guidebook lays out instructions for communities, making an idea that can seem lofty and abstract appear manageable but powerful.

Truth, Racial Healing and Transformation was the vision of a woman named Dr. Gail Christopher. She's an expert in public health and social policy, and she's my mother. At the very end of my three-year journey, I found myself in her home in Prince George's County, Maryland, outside Washington, DC. We sat in a sunroom in the back of the house that she has transformed over the years into a social justice retreat center. She is a small woman with expressive hands and skin that looks like poured honey, even at seventy. Most people who meet her talk about her smile; when she bestows its light on you, you don't soon forget it. She and I were sitting on a cream-colored couch on the day that Congress introduced the resolution calling for a national TRHT, and I asked her why she felt the country needed a Truth, Racial Healing and Transformation effort on top of all the other policies I was advocating for to address inequality.

"It's a powerful, liberating frame to realize that the fallacy of racial hierarchy is a belief system that we don't have to have. We can replace it with another way of looking at each other as human beings. Then, once you get that opening, you invite people to see a new way forward. You ask questions like 'What kind of narrative will your great-grandchildren learn about this country?' 'What is it that will have happened?' Truthfully, we've never done that as a country. We've been dealing with the old model, patching it over here, sticking bubble gum over there." She laughed.

"But we are young. What makes America America is the creative power of our people. It is our responsibility to take this privilege that has come from the exploitation of so many people and the land—to use that freedom to create and actualize the aspirations of tomorrow. We need to envision an America that is no longer bound by that belief in racial hierarchy—we owe it back to the universe. That's bending that moral arc toward justice," she said, and though I'd heard that phrase countless times before, it meant something different to me at the end of my journey.

Dr. King said that the arc of the moral universe is long, but it bends toward justice. But we know that progress is not guaranteed. When the arc in America bends from slavery in the 1860s and returns to convict leasing in the 1880s; when it bends from Jim Crow in the 1960s and returns to mass incarceration in the 1970s; when it bends from Indigenous genocide to an epidemic of Indigenous suicides; when it bends, but as a tree does in the wind, only to sway back, we have to admit that we have not touched the root.

We have not touched the root because the laws we make are expressions of a root belief, and it is time to face our most deep-seated one: the great lie at the root of our nation's founding was a belief in the hierarchy of human value. And we are still there.

This moment is challenging us finally to settle this question: Who is an American, and what are we to one another? We have to admit that this question is harder for us than in most other countries, because we are the world's most radical experiment in democracy, a nation of ancestral strangers that has to work to find connection even as we grow more diverse every day.

But everything depends on the answer to this question. Who is an American, and what are we to one another? Politics offers two visions of why all the peoples of the world have met here: one in which we are nothing more than competitors and another in which perhaps the proximity of so much difference forces us to admit our common humanity.

The choice between these two visions has never been starker. To a nation riven with anxiety about who belongs, many in power have made it their overarching goal to sow distrust about the goodness of the Other. They are holding on, white-knuckled, to a tiny idea of We the People, denying the beauty of what we are becoming. They're warning that demographic changes are the unmaking of America. What I've seen on my journey is that they're the *fulfillment* of America. What they say is a threat is in fact our country's salvation—for when a nation founded on a belief in racial hierarchy truly rejects that belief, then and only then will we have discovered a New World.

That is our destiny. To make it manifest, we must challenge ourselves to live our lives in solidarity across color, origin, and class; we must demand changes to the rules in order to disrupt the very notion that those who have more money are worth more in our democracy and our economy. Since this country's founding, we have not allowed our diversity to be our superpower, and the result is that the United States is not more than the sum of its disparate parts. But it could be. And if it were, all of us would prosper. In short, we must emerge from this crisis in our republic with a new birth of freedom, rooted in the knowledge that we are so much more when the "We" in "We the People" is not some of us, but all of us. We are greater than, and greater for, the sum of us.

ACKNOWLEDGMENTS

Compared to running an organization, folks warned me, living a writer's life would be lonely. To the contrary, this book has been a collaboration from start to finish. I have so many people to thank.

Thank you to the doulas and midwives who supported me most in bringing the original book to life—chief among them Lynn Kanter, who provided invaluable research and writing support from proposal to final copy edit—as well as my agents, Henry Reisch, Tina Bennett, Dorian Karchmar, and Janine Kamouh; my fact-checker, Kelsey Kudak; my friendly but unflinching readers Gina Welch and Donovan X. Ramsey; and my primary research assistants, Aaron Carico and Erin Purdie. The publisher and editor Christopher Jackson at One World believed in this book from day one.

Thank you to the team at Delacorte Press, led by publisher and editor Beverly Horowitz, who helped my dream of reaching young readers become a reality. This dream team included Rebecca Gudelis, Tamar Schwartz, Barbara Perris, Colleen Fellingham, Suzanne Lee, Cathy Bobak, and Tracy Heydweiller. I am deeply grateful to Laura Gardner for reading the manuscript with her precious students in mind.

I would be nowhere without my family: Mom, Dad and Mary, Hassan, Shannon and Ronny, Sadia and Andreas, Taiye and Annie, and the McGhees, Minors, Thayers, Boivins, Shepards, and

Quraeshis. Riaz Shah Hassan Shepard-McGhee, this book is dedicated to your Nana, but it is for you and all the children you'll link arms with as you remake the world. Finally, thank you to my best friend, best editor, and best partner in anything worth doing, Cassim. Your love makes all things possible.

INDEX

Supplemental references are available for download at HeatherMcGhee.com

ABOUT THE AUTHOR

HEATHER MCGHEE designs and promotes solutions to inequality in America. The former president of the inequality-focused think tank Demos, McGhee has drafted legislation, testified before Congress, advised presidential candidates, and contributed regularly to news shows, including NBC's *Meet the Press*. She chairs the board of Color of Change, the nation's largest online racial justice organization. McGhee holds a BA in American studies from Yale University and a JD from the University of California, Berkeley, School of Law. She lives in Brooklyn with her husband and son.

heathermcghee.com
/HeatherCMcGhee
/ @HeatherCMcGhee
/ @hmcghee